Great American Recipes *for* All Seasons

VOLUME 1

Featuring Recipes from the
Southwest & Northeast Regions

Great American Recipes *for* All Seasons

Volume 1 – Featuring Ultrex®

Featuring Recipes from the Southwest & Northeast Regions

Pascoe Publishing, Inc.
Rocklin, California

Cover design by Knockout Books
Page design by Melanie Haage Design

Published in the United States of America by
Pascoe Publishing, Inc.
Rocklin, California
http://www.pascoepublishing.com

ISBN: 1-929862-28-8

03 04 05 06 10 9 8 7 6 5 4 3 2 1

Printed in the United States of America

Table of Contents

Chapter Three: Great American Breads & Breakfast

Chapter Four: Great American Salads & Soups

Chapter Five: Great American Vegetables & Sides

Chapter Six: Great American Entrées

Chapter Seven: Great American Desserts

WELCOME!

From the crisp, invigorating snap of a brisk day in Maine to the sun-soaked delight of a long, colorful sunset in Arizona, cooks in America are inviting the environment in which they live into their very own kitchens. It shows in the regional specialties claimed by chefs in each city and the home-cooked favorites of cooks using local fresh ingredients.

We love experimenting and adopting the special regional foods of America. Inside *Great American Recipes for All Seasons, Volume 1,* we invite you to join us in trying recipes garnered from homemade favorites of the Northeast, as well as tempting and delicious choices from the Southwest.

We hope that you will use your Ultrex® kitchen appliances, bakeware, cookware and accessories when using the recipes inside this book. They are perfect for every baking and cooking project you'll have—no matter where you live!

Visit us at www.hsn.com, keyword, "Ultrex," when you are searching for some exciting Ultrex pieces to add to your collection. And, thank you for inviting us into your home!

Sincerely,

Art & MaryAnn Krull

CHAPTER ONE

Introduction

If you take a moment to think about the foods associated with regions of America, it only takes a few seconds before you will capture a classic recipe and pin it to a geographical area. Clam chowder brings you directly to Boston or Manhattan, maple-syrup glazed ham comes directly from Vermont and salsa calls you to the entire Southwest region. We have a wealth of choices when it comes to selecting recipes from the regions of our country and the recipes inside this book showcase both the tried-and-true classics, as well as new, innovative foods that partner to create regional favorites.

The ever-constant weather patterns of America have much to do with our regional recipe choices. Consider the cold and long winters of the Northeast and you'll recognize that roasted meats, hearty soups and chowders, stews and slow-roasted one-dish dinners are the perfect antidote to a thermostat registering in single digits. The foods of the Northeast are substantial and offer warmth and comfort. Summer in the Northeast also brings tender blueberries and shellfish that are well-known for delicate quality.

Foods of the Southwest are in almost perfect contrast to those of the Northeast—they are typically made using short preparation times by grilling or pan-frying and favor light ingredients such as cilantro, limes and tomatoes. Foods that require baking or roasting are done in the morning, while the kitchens are cool. Soups, such as gazpacho, are served ice-cold in chilled soup bowls. Spices such as cumin, cayenne pepper and chili powder put heat on the tongue, only to be cooled by tortillas or fresh salads.

No matter where you live, you will find inside these pages many delicious and simple-to-prepare dishes that will satisfy all members of your family. Consider *Elegant Seafood-Stuffed Lobster* and *Citrus Teriyaki Tuna* for guests and try *Glazed Maine Wild Blackberry Pie* and *Out-West Chuck Wagon Beef & Bean Chili* for easy family dinners. Each chapter contains recipes from both regions of the country—along with a sprinkling of fusion recipes that highlight the East and the West!

Bon Appetit!

CHAPTER TWO

Great American Appetizers

America inspires every kind of cooking and appetizers are no exception. Almost everyone has a favorite snack, dip or sandwich that accompanies a favorite activity, sport or television program. These recipes are designed to be appropriate for almost any occasion—from elegant cocktail parties to the most informal family evenings—and are indicative of the Northeast and Southwest regions of our country.

For impressive starters, try *Rich Walnut-Ricotta Cheesecake, Chicken & Pear Monte Cristo Appetizer Wedges* or *Walnut & Parmesan Pressed Cheese with Fresh Sage.* Pair a full-bodied red wine with any of these and your most important guests will be delighted.

When you are preparing for an easy family or friends get-together, select *Salsa De Fruta Fresca, Caesar-Style Artichoke Dip* or *Hot-Sauced Shrimp Dip*. Any of these choices will partner well with a casual assortment of vegetables, crackers or peasant-style breads.

Appetizers can be the most creative beginning that makes any meal special, so we invite you to sample and try these recipes and adopt your own favorites!

Chicken & Pear Monte Cristo Appetizer Wedges

2 T. prepared horseradish
8 slices firm white bread
8 slices mozzarella cheese
12 oz. cooked chicken breast, thinly sliced
2 medium Bartlett pears, peeled and thinly sliced
2 large eggs
1/2 c. light cream

Preheat the oven to 350°F. Grease a 10" x 15" baking pan. Spread a thin layer of the horseradish on one side of each of the slices of bread. Layer the cheese, chicken and the pear slices on four slices of bread. Place another layer of cheese and chicken on top of the pear. Top with a slice of bread, horseradish-side down.

In a shallow dish, combine the eggs and the cream. Dip both sides of the sandwiches in the egg mixture. Allow the eggs to absorb into the bread. Place the sandwiches in the prepared pan. Bake for 15 minutes. Using a spatula, turn the sandwiches and bake an additional 10 minutes. To serve, slice each sandwich into wedges and place on a serving platter. Makes 8 servings.

Rich Walnut-Ricotta Cheesecake

- 1 c. walnuts, chopped
- 1/2 c. zwieback toast, crumbled
- 1 T. butter, melted
- 1 1/2 c. feta cheese, crumbled
- 1 t. dried basil
- 15 oz. carton ricotta cheese
- 3 large eggs
- 1/2 c. mushrooms, chopped
- 1/4 c. black olives, chopped
- 1/4 c. lowfat milk
- 1/2 t. ground black pepper
- 1/8 t. salt
- 1/4 c. black olives, sliced (garnish)
- 3 to 4 sprigs fresh oregano (garnish)

Preheat the oven to 325°F. In a medium bowl, mix together the walnuts, zwieback and the butter until blended. Press the walnut mixture into the bottom of a springform pan for the crust. Set aside.

In a large bowl, beat together the feta, basil and ricotta cheese until combined. Add the eggs to the cheese mixture, beating slowly. Add the mushrooms, chopped olives, milk, pepper and salt and stir to combine. Pour the mushrooms and spices into the walnut crust. Place the springform pan in a larger shallow baking pan. Bake for 40 to

45 minutes. Remove the pan and cool for 15 minutes on a wire rack. Use a spatula to separate the edges from the pan. Cool for another 30 minutes. Remove the sides of the springform pan. Cover the cheesecake and refrigerate for 3 hours. To serve, garnish with the sliced olives and a few sprigs of oregano. Makes 20 servings.

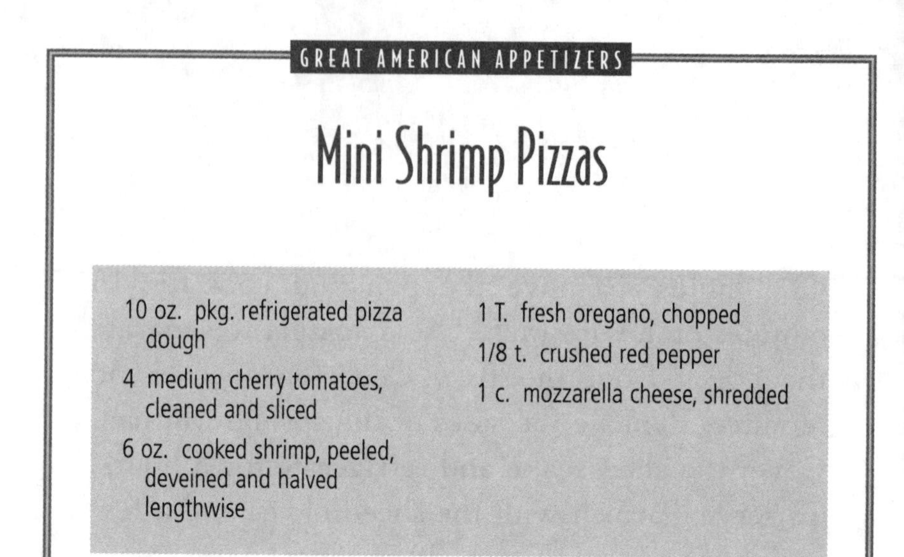

Mini Shrimp Pizzas

- 10 oz. pkg. refrigerated pizza dough
- 4 medium cherry tomatoes, cleaned and sliced
- 6 oz. cooked shrimp, peeled, deveined and halved lengthwise
- 1 T. fresh oregano, chopped
- 1/8 t. crushed red pepper
- 1 c. mozzarella cheese, shredded

Preheat the oven to 425°F. Roll the pizza dough into a 13½" x 9" rectangle on a lightly floured surface. Cut the dough into six 4½-inch squares. Place the squares 1-inch apart on a lightly greased cookie sheet. Bake for 4 to 5 minutes. Remove from the oven and keep the squares on the cookie sheet. On each pizza square, place 3 to 4 tomato slices. Top each square with 4 to 6 pieces of shrimp. Sprinkle the top of the shrimp with oregano and red pepper. Top with the shredded mozzarella cheese. Put the pizza squares back into the oven and bake a few minutes more, until the cheese melts. To serve, place the pizza squares on a serving platter. Makes 6 servings.

Cucumber-Dill Toasted Rounds

- 1 French-style baguette, cut into 1/2-inch slices
- 3 oz. pkg. cream cheese, softened
- 1 t. salt
- 1 t. ground black pepper
- 1/2 t. dried oregano
- 1/2 t. dried basil
- 1/3 c. mayonnaise
- 1 cucumber, peeled and sliced thinly
- 2 t. dried dill weed

Preheat the oven to 350°F. Place the slices of baguette on a cookie sheet. Bake the slices of bread for 3 minutes; turn and bake another 3 minutes, until the baguette slices are golden and toasted. Set aside.

In a medium bowl, mix together the cream cheese, salt, pepper, oregano, basil and mayonnaise. Spread a thin layer of the cream cheese on the toasted baguette slices. Top each slice of toast with a slice of cucumber. Sprinkle the cucumber with the dill. To serve, place the toasted baguette slices on a platter. Makes 12 servings.

Savory Ham & Chutney-Stuffed Mushrooms

- 1 c. cooked ham, finely diced
- 1 1/2 T. Dijon mustard
- 1 T. chutney, minced
- 2 t. cider vinegar
- 2 green onions, finely diced
- 1/2 c. sour cream
- 1 T. mayonnaise
- 14 medium mushrooms, cleaned and stemmed

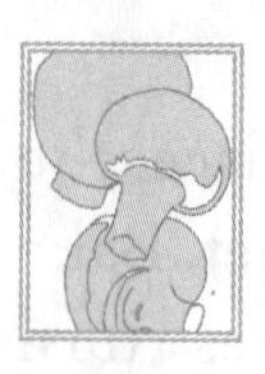

In a medium mixing bowl, blend together the ham, mustard, chutney, vinegar, green onions, sour cream and mayonnaise until well blended. Mound the stuffing into the mushroom caps, packing lightly and arrange on a serving platter. Cover with plastic wrap and chill until ready to serve. Makes 4 to 6 servings.

Romano & Sweet Onion-Stuffed Portobello

- 1/3 c. sweet onion, chopped
- 1/2 t. brown sugar
- 1/2 t. extra virgin olive oil
- 1/2 c. firm tofu, crumbled
- 1 t. salt
- 1 large Portobello mushroom, cleaned and dried
- 1/4 c. Romano cheese, grated
- 1/4 t. ground nutmeg
- fresh parsley, chopped

Preheat the oven to 350°F. Over medium-low heat, sauté the onion and sugar in the olive oil, until the onion is transparent. Add the tofu and salt. Cook until the tofu is lightly browned. Remove the pan from the heat. Place the mushroom on a baking sheet, stem-side up. Cover the stem-side of the mushroom with the tofu filling. Sprinkle the filling with the cheese and nutmeg. Bake for 10 to 15 minutes on the middle rack of the oven. Remove from the heat. To serve, cut the mushroom into wedges and sprinkle with the fresh parsley. Makes 4 servings.

Walnut & Parmesan Pressed Cheese with Fresh Sage

- 3 cloves garlic, skinned
- 1 c. ricotta cheese
- 1/2 c. Gorgonzola cheese, crumbled
- 1 c. whipping cream
- 1 t. salt
- 2 leaves fresh sage
- 1/2 c. walnuts, chopped
- Parmesan cheese for topping

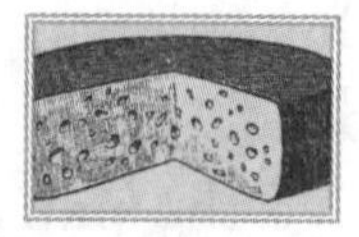

Cook the garlic in boiling water until soft, 15 to 20 minutes. Place the garlic in a press and press out 2 tablespoons of juice. Discard the garlic and set the juice aside.

In a medium bowl, beat the ricotta cheese with an electric mixer until soft. Add the Gorgonzola and blend on medium speed until smooth, about 2 minutes. Beat in the cream, salt and the 2 tablespoons of garlic juice. Dampen a 12" x 18" piece of cheesecloth and wring it dry. Lay the sage leaves down, bottom-side up, in the center of the cheesecloth. Spread the cheese evenly over the leaves. Tie the ends of the cheesecloth together, pressing the cheese into the shape of a ball.

Place the cheesecloth-covered cheese ball in a large strainer. Set the strainer over a large bowl and refrigerate for 24 hours. Remove the cheesecloth from the molded cheese and place the cheese ball on a serving platter. Press the walnuts over the entire surface of the cheese ball and sprinkle with Parmesan cheese. Serve with an assorted selection of crackers. Makes 6 to 8 servings.

Fruit Skewers with Cream Cheese Dip

1/3 c. sour cream
8 oz. pkg. cream cheese, cubed
1/4 c. powdered sugar
1 T. orange juice concentrate
1 T. lime juice
2 T. marshmallow cream
1/2 c. whipping cream
3 c. angel food cake, cubed
3 c. strawberries, blueberries, cantaloupe chunks, pineapple chunks, seedless grapes
12 12-inch wooden skewers

In a small mixing bowl, blend the sour cream, cream cheese, powdered sugar, orange juice, lime juice and marshmallow cream until very smooth. Add the whipping cream and mix until blended and creamy. Cover and chill.

Prepare skewers of the assorted fruit, alternating with the cake pieces in between. Place a grape on each end of the skewers. To serve, offer the chilled dip as an accompaniment to the fruit and cake skewers. Makes 12 servings.

Golden Brown Asparagus Rolls

1/2 c. blue cheese

1/4 c. feta cheese

1 c. cream cheese, softened

1 egg

1 loaf sliced white bread, no crust

10 fresh asparagus spears, cleaned, trimmed and dried (you may substitute frozen, thawed asparagus, if desired)

1/2 c. melted butter

In a medium bowl, mix together with an electric mixer the blue cheese, feta cheese, cream cheese and egg until the mixture is smooth and spreadable. Roll out with a rolling pin each slice of bread until flat and spread each with the cheese mixture. Place one spear of asparagus on each slice and roll tightly. Secure the rolls with a toothpick, if needed. Place the bread rolls in plastic resealable bags and freeze for at least 4 hours or up to 6 hours.

Preheat the oven to 350°F. Remove the rolls from the freezer and place them on a large baking sheet. Remove any toothpicks. Brush each bread roll with the melted butter. Bake for 10 minutes, or until the bread rolls are a golden brown. To serve, place on a platter and serve warm. Makes 10 servings.

Caesar-Style Artichoke Dip

- 1/2 c. Caesar-style salad dressing
- 1/4 c. mayonnaise
- 1/2 c. sour cream
- 2/3 c. Parmesan cheese, grated
- 2/3 c. Swiss cheese, shredded
- 14 oz. can artichoke hearts, drained
- 1 c. ripe tomatoes, chopped

Preheat the oven to 350°F. In a medium bowl, combine the Caesar-style dressing, mayonnaise, sour cream and Parmesan cheese until well blended. Add the Swiss cheese, artichoke hearts and the tomatoes. Stir to mix well. Lightly coat a square baking dish 8" x 8" with nonstick cooking spray and pour the dip into the dish. Bake for 40 to 45 minutes, or until bubbly and heated through. Serve hot with your choice of crackers. Makes 24 servings.

Cold Shrimp with Fruit & Curry Sauce

- 4 T. butter
- 1 small yellow onion, chopped
- 1 small apple, peeled and chopped
- 1/2 banana, chopped
- 2 T. mango chutney
- 1 t. curry powder
- 1 c. chicken broth
- 1 lb. cooked shrimp, cleaned and deveined

In a large skillet over medium heat melt the butter. Add the onion, apple, banana, chutney and the curry powder. Cook for 3 minutes until the onion is translucent. Add the chicken broth to the skillet and bring it to a boil. Reduce the heat to low and simmer for an additional 5 minutes. Remove the skillet from the heat. In a blender puree the fruit mixture until smooth. Return the fruit sauce to the skillet and heat until it is just hot. Pour the sauce into a bowl, cover and refrigerate. To serve, place the bowl on a platter and surround it with the shrimp. Provide a spoon for the sauce. Makes 4 to 6 servings.

Bacon, Tomato & Cheese-Filled Biscuits

10 slices bacon
1 medium tomato, chopped
1/2 yellow onion, chopped
1/2 c. Monterey Jack cheese, shredded
1/3 c. mayonnaise
1 t. dried basil
1 can buttermilk biscuit dough (6 biscuits)

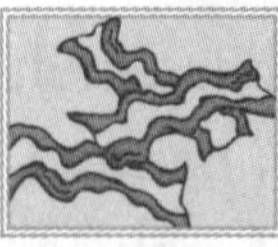

Preheat the oven to 375°F. Lightly grease 12 muffin cups. In a skillet, cook the bacon over medium heat until brown. Place the bacon on paper towels to absorb the fat. Crumble the bacon into a medium bowl when cool. Add the tomato, onion, cheese, mayonnaise and basil. Mix thoroughly. Set aside.

Separate the buttermilk biscuits into halves. Place each biscuit half in the prepared muffin pan, pressing the dough halfway up the sides of the cup. Fill each biscuit half with the bacon mixture. Bake for 10 to 12 minutes until the muffins are lightly golden. Remove the pans from the oven and cool for 5 minutes on a wire rack. Remove the biscuits to a wire rack to cool. To serve, place the individual biscuits on a serving platter. Makes 12 servings.

Jalapeño & Garden Vegetable Dip

29 oz. can pumpkin puree
8 oz. pkg. cream cheese, softened
1 T. juice from pickled jalapeños
1 c. sour cream
4 oz. can diced green chilies
1 clove garlic, minced
1 medium ripe tomato, chopped
4 oz. can sliced black olives
2 green onions, chopped
1/3 c. red onion, chopped

In a large bowl, mix together the pumpkin, cream cheese and the jalapeño juice until well blended. Lightly coat an 8-inch square serving dish. Spread the pumpkin mixture evenly into the dish. In a smaller bowl, mix the sour cream, green chilies and garlic. Layer the sour cream over the pumpkin and smooth with a knife. Top with the tomato, olives, green onions and red onions. Cover and refrigerate until chilled, about 1 hour. Serve with tortilla chips. Makes 12 servings.

Fresh Chive & Dijon Deviled Eggs

24 large hard-cooked eggs
3/4 c. sour cream
1/4 c. mayonnaise
1/4 c. fresh chives, chopped
1/4 t. red pepper sauce
1 T. Dijon mustard
2 t. fresh lemon juice
1/2 t. ground black pepper
1/2 c. ham, cooked and chopped

Peel the eggs and cut in half lengthwise. Scoop out the egg yolks into a large bowl. Chop 4 egg white halves and add them to the bowl of yolks. Set aside the remaining egg whites.

Into the bowl of egg yolks, add the sour cream, mayonnaise, chives, red pepper sauce, mustard, lemon juice and black pepper. Mash with a fork until smooth. Fill the reserved egg white halves with the yolk mixture. Place the filled eggs on a platter. Top each egg with ¼ teaspoon chopped ham. Refrigerate prior to serving and refrigerate any leftovers. Makes 20 servings.

Salsa de Fruta Fresca

- 1 large tomato, halved
- 1 ripe mango, peeled and sliced
- 1 ripe orange, peeled and sliced
- 2 ripe kiwis, peeled and sliced
- 1 small red onion, quartered
- 1 ripe avocado, sliced
- 1 jalapeño chile pepper (optional)
- 1 clove garlic, minced
- 1 t. ground black pepper

In a blender, mix the tomato, mango, orange, kiwis, red onion, avocado, chili pepper, garlic and black pepper using the pulse setting. Blend until the ingredients are finely chopped with some pieces of fruit visible. Chill the salsa at least 1 hour. To serve, spoon the salsa into a bowl and provide blue corn tortilla chips for dipping. Makes 4 cups.

Hot-Sauced Shrimp Dip

- 8 oz. pkg. cream cheese, softened
- 1 t. Worcestershire sauce
- 2 t. bottled hot sauce
- 1 c. cocktail sauce
- 12 oz. cooked shrimp, rinsed, deveined and tails removed
- 1 green onion, chopped
- 1 yellow onion, chopped
- 1 ripe tomato, chopped
- 1 c. mozzarella cheese, shredded

In a medium bowl, combine the cream cheese, Worcestershire sauce and the hot sauce until blended and smooth. Spread the cream cheese mixture on a medium serving platter and top with the cocktail sauce. Layer the shrimp over the cocktail sauce. Garnish the shrimp with the green onion, yellow onion, tomato and the shredded mozzarella cheese. Serve with round butter crackers or crunchy flatbread. Makes 3½ cups.

Flaky Baked Brie with Nuts

1/2 package frozen puff pastry	1/3 c. almonds, sliced
1 round Brie cheese	1/4 c. walnuts, chopped

Preheat the oven to 350°F. Cut the Brie horizontally creating two rounds of thinner cheese. Place the thawed puff pastry in a pie pan, arranging the pastry evenly in the pan. Place one half of the Brie on the pastry dough. Sprinkle the almonds and walnuts over the top of the cheese. Place the other round of cheese on top of the nuts, making sure that both rounds are rind out. Wrap the pastry dough around the Brie. Place the pie pan in the oven and bake for 15 to 20 minutes. Remove the cheese from the oven and allow the Brie to cool for 5 minutes before serving. To serve, place the baked Brie on a serving platter. Place crackers or vegetables alongside. Cut the flaky Brie into thin wedges. Provide a spoon for the cheese. Makes 9 servings.

Classic Hush Puppies

1 1/2 c. all-purpose flour	1/2 t. salt
3/4 c. yellow cornmeal	2 large eggs
2 t. baking powder	3/4 c. buttermilk
1 1/2 t. baking soda	4 c. canola or vegetable oil

In a large mixing bowl, combine the flour, cornmeal, baking powder, baking soda and the salt and mix well. In a separate bowl, whisk together the eggs and the buttermilk. Add the egg mixture to the flour mixture and stir just until moistened. The cornmeal mixture will be lumpy.

Heat the oil in a deep saucepan or deep fryer over medium-high heat until it reaches 375°F. Drop large teaspoonfuls of the cornmeal batter into the hot oil, a few at a time. Do not overcrowd. Fry until the hush puppies are golden brown, turning twice. Transfer the hush puppies to paper towels to drain. To serve, mound the hush puppies on a platter. Serve as an appetizer with an assortment of dips, including marinara, ranch dip or tartar sauce or serve as an accompaniment to fried fish or chicken. Makes about 3 dozen hush puppies.

Lime & Avocado Vegetable Dip

- 1 c. plain yogurt
- 1/4 c. sour cream
- 1 large avocado, peeled and chopped
- 1 shallot, chopped
- 1 green onion, chopped
- 1/2 c. red onion, chopped
- 1/2 t. dried tarragon
- pinch dried oregano
- 2 T. fresh lime juice
- salt and pepper to taste

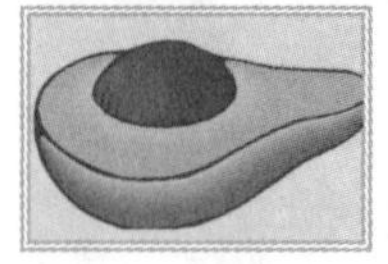

In a blender container, place the yogurt, sour cream, avocado, shallot, green onion, red onion, tarragon, oregano, lime juice and the salt and pepper. Blend until very smooth. Serve immediately with fresh vegetables or assorted crackers. Makes 4 to 6 servings.

CHAPTER THREE

Great American Breads & Breakfast

Breakfast is a favorite meal in America, calling to mind the most alluring aromas—bacon frying, cinnamon bread baking and ripe berries piled with rich cream. We revel in the time spent over breakfast and Americans cherish the weekend mornings when a special breakfast can be accompanied by a slow perusal through the morning newspaper.

The Northeast region of America invites specialty recipes that have been, in some cases, handed down through several generations of cooks. With an emphasis on hearty foods and preparation of local produce, the region is marked additionally by the pure and divine maple syrup that comes from Vermont. It's almost impossible to skip breakfast in the Northeast—there are simply too many delicious choices!

The Southwest region of America also brings to

mind a vast array of specialty breakfast foods. Most are prepared quickly and often include a touch of jalapeño or chili powder for a wake-up bite first thing in the morning! Fresh tomato salsas are popular with just about any breakfast foods, as are fruit salsas and accompaniments.

It goes without saying that breads are an important part of the American culture, wherever you live. We all have one or two special family recipes tucked away that may evoke memories of another homeland—Germany, Italy, England, Mexico and many more. We share in this chapter some of the recipes that are particularly special to the Southwest and Northeast regions of America, however they are *so* delicious that they'll have no boundaries among those who indulge in sharing them.

Bacon & Egg Breakfast Pitas

3 slices Canadian bacon, diced
3 eggs
1 T. chives, minced
1 whole-wheat pita bread
1/4 c. cheddar cheese, grated

In a skillet over medium heat, brown the Canadian bacon. Place the cooked bacon on a paper towel to remove any excess fat. In a small bowl, lightly mix the eggs and chives. Return the skillet to the heat and scramble the eggs and the Canadian bacon together until set. Top the egg and bacon combination with cheddar cheese.

In a separate skillet, warm the pita bread on low. Remove the pita from the skillet and cut it in half. Fill each half with the egg and bacon scramble. Serve warm. Makes 2 servings.

New York Soft Pretzels

3 c. all-purpose flour
1 T. sugar
2 t. salt
2 t. baking powder
2 t. active dry yeast
2 T. unsalted butter, melted
1 c. warm water, 110-115°F
8 c. water
4 t. baking soda
1 egg, beaten
2 t. coarse salt

In a large mixing bowl, stir together the flour, sugar, salt, baking powder and yeast. Add the butter and the 1 cup warm water to make a soft dough. Turn out onto a lightly floured board and knead until smooth, about 10 minutes. Place the dough in a buttered bowl, turn to coat the dough and cover the bowl with a clean cloth. Place the bowl in a warm spot, and allow to double in size, about 2 hours.

Punch down the dough and on a lightly floured board, divide the dough into 8 equal pieces. Roll or cut each piece into a rope 18 to 20 inches long, and twist each rope into a pretzel shape. Cover the pretzels and allow them to rise for 30 minutes in a warm place.

Preheat the oven to 400°F. In a large pot, boil 8 cups of water and add the baking soda. Slide a few of the pretzels into the boiling water at a time with a slotted spoon or broad spatula, and boil each one until they float to the top. Carefully turn over each pretzel once. Remove the boiled pretzels from the water and place them on a lightly greased cookie sheet. Brush the tops of each pretzel with the beaten egg and sprinkle with coarse salt. Bake 10 to 15 minutes until golden. Remove the pretzels from the oven and cool on wire racks. Makes 8 thick pretzels.

Hearty Fruit & Almond Granola

- 2 ripe bananas, peeled
- 1 c. raisins
- 1/4 c. dark brown sugar, packed
- 1/4 c. hot water
- 1 T. vanilla extract
- 1 t. ground cinnamon
- 8 c. quick oats
- 1 c. dried mixed fruit
- 1 c. roasted almonds, slivered

Preheat the oven to 250°F. Using a food processor, blend the bananas, raisins, brown sugar, hot water, vanilla and cinnamon until mixed well. Transfer the fruit to a large bowl. Add the oatmeal and mix well. Spread the oatmeal mixture on a 10" x 15" baking sheet and bake for 1 hour, stirring every 10 minutes as the granola bakes. Remove the baking sheet from the oven and allow the granola to cool. Stir in the dried fruit and almonds. Allow the granola to cool completely and transfer into an airtight container. Makes 20 servings.

Zesty Cranberry Crunch Bread

- 1 c. all-purpose flour
- 1 1/2 c. crushed graham crackers
- 1/3 c. dark brown sugar, packed
- 2 t. baking powder
- 1/2 t. salt
- 1 c. dried cranberries
- 1/2 c walnuts, chopped
- 2 t. orange zest
- 1 egg, lightly beaten
- 1 c. fresh orange juice
- 1/4 c. vegetable oil

Preheat the oven to 350°F. Grease a 9" x 5" loaf pan. In a large mixing bowl, blend together the flour, graham cracker crumbs, brown sugar, baking powder and the salt. Stir in the cranberries, walnuts and orange zest thoroughly. Add the beaten egg, orange juice and the oil. Stir until completely blended. Spread the bread evenly into the prepared pan. Bake for 1 hour. When the bread is done, a toothpick inserted in the center will come out clean. Remove the pan from the oven and cool the bread in the pan for 15 minutes. Transfer the bread to a wire rack to cool thoroughly. Slice and serve or wrap tightly in plastic wrap. Makes 12 servings.

Breakfast Potatoes & Ham Quiche

4 c. russet potatoes, peeled and shredded
1/4 c. butter or margarine, melted
1 1/2 t. seasoned salt
1 c. ham, cooked and diced
1/4 c. red onion, diced
1/2 c. button mushrooms, cleaned and diced
1 c. cheddar cheese, shredded
2 eggs
1/2 c. whole milk
1/2 t. salt
1/4 t. ground black pepper

Preheat the oven to 425°F. Cover the bottom and sides of a 9-inch pie dish with the shredded potatoes. Drizzle the melted butter over the potatoes. Sprinkle the seasoned salt over the melted butter. Bake for 20 minutes, remove from the heat and set aside.

Reduce the oven to 350°F. In a medium bowl, combine the ham, onion, mushrooms and the cheese. In a separate bowl, whisk together the eggs, milk, salt and black pepper until blended. Spread the ham and vegetables over the cooked potato crust. Cover the ham with the egg mixture.

Bake for 20 to 25 minutes, or until the quiche has become puffy and golden brown. Remove the quiche from the oven and serve warm. Makes 6 servings.

Baked Orange, Apple & Cinnamon Breakfast Puff

- 1/2 c. evaporated milk
- 1/3 c. all-purpose baking mix
- 3 T. sugar, divided
- 3 eggs, yolks and whites separated
- 1 T. orange juice
- 1 T. ground cinnamon
- 1 apple, peeled, cored and sliced thinly
- ground cinnamon and sugar for garnish

Grease a 10-inch ovenproof skillet. Preheat the oven to 375°F. and place the skillet in the oven to preheat. In a food processor, pour the evaporated milk, baking mix, 1 tablespoon sugar, egg yolks, orange juice and the cinnamon. Blend the mixture until smooth. In a separate mixing bowl, beat the egg whites until peaks begin to form. Gradually add to the egg whites the remaining sugar and beat until stiff peaks form. Gently fold in the evaporated milk mixture. Pour the batter into the preheated skillet. Push each apple slice ½-inch into the batter creating a windmill pattern.

Sprinkle with cinnamon and a little sugar to garnish. Bake for 10 to 15 minutes, or until the puff is golden and baked through. Serve immediately. Makes 6 to 8 servings.

Apple Spice & Cheddar Bread

- 2/3 c. sugar
- 2 c. self-rising flour
- 1 t. ground cinnamon
- 1/3 c. walnuts, chopped
- 1 medium red apple, cored, peeled and chopped
- 3/4 c. cheddar cheese, shredded
- 2 eggs, lightly beaten
- 1/3 c. butter, melted
- 1/4 c. whole milk

Preheat the oven to 350°F. Grease a 9" x 5" loaf pan. In a large bowl, combine the sugar, flour, cinnamon, walnuts, apples and cheese. Mix in the eggs, melted butter and the milk. Stir the batter until it is well blended and all of the dry ingredients are well-incorporated. Pour the bread batter into the prepared pan. Bake for 1 hour. If the loaf begins to brown too quickly, cover the top of the loaf with aluminum foil. The bread is done when a toothpick inserted in the center comes out clean. Remove the bread from the oven and cool in the pan for 10 minutes on a wire rack. Transfer the bread to the wire rack and finish cooling. Slice and serve or wrap tightly in plastic wrap. Makes 12 servings.

Pastel de Chile Relleno

- 4 eggs, beaten
- 1/2 c. milk
- 1 small red bell pepper, diced
- 1/4 t. salt
- 1/8 t. ground black pepper
- 1/2 c. cheddar cheese
- 1/2 c. pepperjack cheese
- 4 oz. can diced green chilies
- 1 ripe tomatillo, diced
- 1 prepared 9-inch piecrust
- sour cream for garnish
- salsa for garnish

Preheat the oven to 350°F. Combine the beaten eggs, milk, red bell pepper, salt, pepper, cheeses, chilies and the tomatillo in a large bowl. Mix thoroughly. Pour the chile rellano into the pie shell. Bake for 45 to 50 minutes, or until the chile rellano is firm and lightly golden on top. Remove the chile rellano from the oven and let it stand until just warm. To serve, cut into 6 wedges and garnish each serving with a spoonful of sour cream and salsa. Makes 6 servings.

Italian Ricotta & Parmesan Zucchini Quiche

- 4 slices sourdough bread
- 1 T. butter
- 1 c. zucchini, sliced thin
- 1 large tomato, chopped
- 1 t. fresh oregano, chopped
- 2 T. all-purpose flour
- 1 c. ricotta cheese
- 2 eggs, beaten
- 3/4 c. sour cream
- 1/2 c. Parmesan cheese, grated and divided

Preheat the oven to 375°F. Slice the bread diagonally into halves, making 8 triangles total. In a 9-inch pie plate, arrange the bread around edges. Set aside.

In a skillet over medium-high heat, melt the butter and sauté the zucchini until tender. Add the tomatoes and the oregano and cook for 3 minutes more. Stir in the flour and then transfer the mixture to the pie plate.

In a separate bowl, combine the ricotta cheese, eggs, sour cream and ¼-cup of the Parmesan cheese. Pour the cheese and eggs over the vegetables and sprinkle the remaining Parmesan cheese over all evenly. Bake for 30 minutes, or until a knife inserted in the center comes out clean. Remove the quiche from the oven, cool for 10 minutes and serve. Makes 6 servings.

Pumpkin Pecan Waffles

2 c. all-purpose flour
1/4 c. sugar
1 T. cornstarch
2 t. baking powder
1 1/2 t. ground cinnamon
1/2 t. salt
1/4 t. ground nutmeg
2 eggs
1 1/3 c. light cream
1/2 c. canned pumpkin puree
2 T. butter, melted
1/2 c. pecans, chopped
1/2 c. walnuts, chopped

Preheat the waffle iron according to the appliance directions. In a large mixing bowl, mix together the flour, sugar, cornstarch, baking powder, cinnamon, salt and nutmeg. Separate the egg whites and yolks. In a medium bowl, combine the egg yolks with the cream and the pumpkin until smooth. Add the pumpkin and cream to the dry ingredients. Add the butter and blend again. In a separate bowl, beat the egg whites until peaks form. Gently fold the egg whites into the pumpkin. Pour the batter onto the waffle iron as directed by the owner's manual. Sprinkle the batter with the nuts. Bake in the waffle iron until the waffle is ready. Serve hot. Makes 4 servings.

Sunny Orange Breakfast Bread

- 1 loaf frozen bread dough, thawed
- 2 T. butter
- 1/2 c. sugar
- 1/2 c. walnuts, chopped
- 1 t. orange zest
- 1/2 c. powdered sugar
- 1 1/2 T. fresh orange juice
- 1 t. fresh lemon juice
- 1/4 t. orange zest

Preheat the oven to 275°F. Grease a 10"x 15" jellyroll baking pan. Press the bread dough into the jelly roll pan, smoothing with your fingers to evenly spread the dough. Spread the butter onto the bread and poke the bread with a fork in several places. In a small bowl, combine the sugar, walnuts and the zest. Sprinkle the sugar mixture over the dough. Bake for 15 minutes.

While the bread is baking, combine in a small bowl the powdered sugar, orange juice, lemon juice and zest to make a glaze. Remove the bread from the oven and drizzle the glaze over the bread. Let the bread stand for 5 minutes and then cut. Serve warm. Makes 10 servings.

Quick & Easy Banana Bread

3 ripe bananas	2 eggs
2 c. all-purpose baking mix	1/2 c. sugar

Preheat the oven to 350°F. Grease a 9"x 5" loaf pan. In a large bowl, mash the bananas with a fork. Add the baking mix, sugar and the eggs. Mix until blended well. Pour the bread batter into the loaf pan and smooth evenly with a knife. Bake for 50 to 60 minutes, or until a toothpick inserted in the center comes out clean. Remove the pan from the oven and let it stand for 10 minutes. Transfer the bread to a wire rack and cool completely. Slice and serve or wrap tightly with plastic wrap. Makes 10 servings.

Blackberry & Pecan French Toast

- 1/4 c. butter
- 1/2 c. dark brown sugar, packed
- 3 T. dark corn syrup
- 1/2 c. pecans, chopped
- 4 eggs
- 1/2 c. light cream
- 1 t. vanilla extract
- 1 loaf French bread, cut into 2-inch slices
- whipped cream
- 1 c. fresh blackberries, rinsed and drained

In a small saucepan over low heat, cook the butter, brown sugar and corn syrup until bubbles form. Pour the sugars into a 9" x 13" nonstick baking dish. Sprinkle the pecans over the sugars. Layer the French bread slices over the sugar and pecans. In a medium bowl, beat together the eggs, cream and vanilla until well blended. Pour the egg and cream over the bread slices. Cover and refrigerate for 1 hour.

Preheat the oven to 350°F. Bake the chilled French toast for 45 minutes. Remove the pan from the oven. Carefully invert the pan upside down onto a serving platter until the bread slides out. Serve garnished with whipped cream and fresh blackberries. Serves 6.

Chorizo Sausage & Red Onion Scramble

2 t. butter
2 T. red onions, chopped
15 oz. can tomato sauce
1/4 lb. Chorizo sausage
1 pinch ground red pepper
8 eggs
3 T. milk
salt and pepper to taste

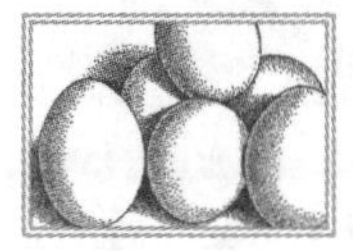

In a skillet over medium heat, melt the butter. Sauté the onion in the butter until the onion is tender and translucent. Add the chorizo to the skillet and cook until it is browned. Crumble the sausage into uniform pieces as it cooks. Add the tomato sauce and red pepper to the skillet. Simmer on low heat for 10 minutes.

In a small bowl, whisk together the eggs and milk. In another skillet over medium-high heat, cook the eggs adding salt and pepper to taste. To serve, place the scrambled eggs on a platter and ladle the chorizo sauce over the top. Serve the extra chorizo sauce alongside. Makes 4 servings.

Maine Blueberry Breakfast Cake

- 1/2 c. butter, softened
- 1/2 c. sugar
- 2 eggs
- 3/4 c. all-purpose flour
- 1 t. ground cinnamon
- 3 c. fresh blueberries, rinsed and drained (you may substitute frozen, thawed and drained blueberries, if desired)
- 1 c. sour cream
- 1/4 c. sugar
- 1 egg white

Preheat the oven to 350°F. Grease and flour a 9-inch springform pan. In a medium bowl, cream together with an electric mixer on medium speed the butter and ½-cup sugar until fluffy. Add the eggs one at a time, mixing continuously. In a separate bowl, mix together the flour and cinnamon. Add the flour slowly to the creamed mixture and beat until smooth. Add ½-cup of the blueberries and fold gently to blend. Pour the batter into the prepared pan. Pour the remaining blueberries over the top of the batter. Bake for 25 to 30 minutes, or until a toothpick inserted in the center comes out clean.

In a medium bowl, beat together the sour cream, sugar and egg white. Remove the cake from the oven, and carefully spread the sour cream topping over the cake. Bake for 10 additional minutes. Remove the pan from the oven and cool on a rack for 30 minutes. Remove the springform sides and place the coffeecake on a serving platter. Makes 8 servings.

Apricot Jam Coffeecake

Topping:

2/3 c. all-purpose flour

1/2 c. dark brown sugar, packed

1 c. almonds, slivered

1/2 c. unsalted butter, chilled and cut into pieces

Coffeecake:

2 c. all-purpose flour

1/2 t. baking soda

1 t. baking powder

1/2 c. unsalted butter, softened

1/2 c. sugar

2 eggs

1 c. apricot jam

3/4 c. buttermilk

In a food processor, combine the flour, brown sugar, almonds and the chilled butter, pulsing until the mixture resembles coarse crumbs. Set aside.

Preheat the oven to 350°F. Grease and flour a 9" x 13" baking pan. In a large mixing bowl, combine the flour, baking soda and baking powder. In a separate bowl, cream together with an electric mixer the butter and sugar until fluffy. Add the eggs to the butter and sugar, one at a time, mixing continuously. Add the apricot jam and continue mixing. Mix in half of the flour just until blended, and add the buttermilk. Add the remaining flour mixture and beat until smooth. Spread the coffeecake batter into the prepared pan. Sprinkle the topping over the batter and pat gently. Bake for 40 to 50 minutes, or until a toothpick inserted in the center comes out clean. Remove from the oven and cool on a rack for 25 minutes before serving. Makes 12 servings.

"Good Morning" Apple Coffeecake

- 3/4 c. butter, softened
- 1 c. Neufchatel cheese, softened
- 1 1/2 c. sugar, divided
- 2 eggs
- 1 3/4 c. all-purpose flour
- 1 t. baking powder
- 1/2 t. baking soda
- 1/4 t. salt
- 1/3 c. whole milk
- 2 T. all-purpose flour
- 2 t. ground cinnamon
- 2 T. lemon juice
- 4 c. tart green apples, peeled and thinly sliced

Preheat the oven to 350°F. Grease a 9" x 13" baking pan. In a large bowl, cream together the butter and the Neufchatel cheese until smooth. Add 1 cup of sugar to the creamed mixture and beat together until light and fluffy. Add the eggs one at a time, mixing continuously. In a separate bowl, combine the 1¾ cup of flour, baking powder, baking soda and the salt. Add the dry ingredients to the butter and cheese, along with the milk. Mix thoroughly until no lumps remain. Transfer the batter to the prepared baking pan.

In a small bowl, combine the remaining ½-cup sugar, the 2 tablespoons flour and the cinnamon. Set aside. Dip the apple slices into the lemon juice.

Coat the apple slices with the cinnamon mixture and place the slices on top of the coffeecake batter. Bake for 50 to 60 minutes. A toothpick inserted in the center of the coffeecake will come out clean when the cake is done. Remove the cake to a wire rack to cool for 10 minutes. Cut and serve warm. Makes 8 servings.

Two Cheese & Asparagus Breakfast Casserole

- 1 lb. ground pork sausage
- 12 eggs
- 10 3/4 oz. can condensed cream of asparagus soup
- 1 1/2 c. milk
- 15 oz. can cut asparagus, drained
- 6 oz. can sliced mushrooms, drained
- 12 oz. package frozen potato rounds
- 1/4 c. cheddar cheese, grated
- 1/4 c. Monterey Jack cheese, grated

Preheat the oven to 350°F. Grease a 9" x 13" baking pan. In a skillet over medium heat, cook the sausage until brown. Crumble the sausage into even pieces with a fork as it cooks. Drain off any excess fat and set aside. In a large bowl, whisk together the eggs, soup and the milk. Stir in the cooked sausage, mushrooms and the asparagus and pour into the prepared pan. Place the frozen potatoes on top of the casserole. Bake for 50 minutes. Sprinkle both cheeses on top of the potatoes and bake an additional 10 minutes. Remove the pan from the oven, cool 10 minutes, cut into squares and serve. Makes 12 servings.

Peach & Toasted Almond Coffee Cake

- 1/2 c. all-purpose flour
- 1/2 c. toasted almonds, finely chopped
- 1/4 c. dark brown sugar, packed
- 1/4 t. ground nutmeg
- 1/4 c. mayonnaise
- 2 c. dry pound cake mix
- 1/3 c. whole milk
- 2 eggs
- 16 oz. can sliced peaches, drained

Preheat the oven to 350°F. Grease a 9" x 13" baking pan. In a medium bowl, mix together the flour, almonds, brown sugar and the nutmeg. Stir in the mayonnaise until the flour mixture resembles small crumbs. Set aside.

In large bowl, beat the cake mix, milk and the eggs until blended well. Spread the cake into the prepared baking pan. Layer the peaches on top of the cake batter. Top the peaches with the almond crumbs, sprinkling evenly across the cake. Bake for 60 minutes. Remove the pan from the oven and cool for 15 minutes on a rack. Serve warm. Makes 12 servings.

Spicy Artichoke & Salsa Omelet

1 c. prepared salsa	2 c. cheddar cheese, shredded
1 1/4 c. artichoke hearts, chopped	6 large eggs
1 green onion, chopped	1 c. plain yogurt
1 small yellow onion, chopped	sour cream for garnish

Preheat the oven to 400°F. Pour the salsa into a 9-inch greased pie plate. Layer the artichoke hearts and both onions on top of the salsa. Sprinkle the onions with the cheddar cheese. In a medium bowl, mix together the eggs and yogurt until well blended. Pour the egg mixture over the cheese layer. Bake for 30 to 40 minutes, or until a knife inserted in the center comes out clean. Remove from the oven and cool on a wire rack for 10 minutes. To serve, cut the omelet into wedges, and top with sour cream and additional salsa, if desired. Makes 6 servings.

Baked Grapefruit Bowls

- 2 red grapefruits
- 2 Minneola oranges, without seeds
- 1 banana, sliced
- 1 apple, sliced
- 1/3 c. raisins
- 1 T. butter
- 2 T. light brown sugar
- 1/2 t. ground cinnamon

Preheat the oven to 450°F. Cut each grapefruit in half. Cut a small sliver from the bottom of the grapefruit halves so that they will sit flat. Place the grapefruit halves in a 3-qt. baking dish. Use a grapefruit knife to cut around the outer edge and between each grapefruit section. In a medium bowl, combine the orange slices, banana slices, apples and the raisins. Top each grapefruit half with the fruit mixture. Cut a small piece of butter and place it on top of each fruit mound. In a small bowl, combine the brown sugar and cinnamon and sprinkle over the fruit. Place in the oven and bake uncovered for 12 minutes. Remove the baking dish and serve immediately. Makes 4 servings.

CHAPTER FOUR

Great American Salads & Soups

Beyond a simple green lettuce salad or a classic cole slaw, a much bigger world of salads exist. None are better than those that have evolved from years of living in regions of America and taking advantage of regional produce, herbs and spices.

In the Northeast, you will find berries in abundance during the summer months, tender lettuces in the summer and firm squash in the harvest months. In the Southwest, the growing season extends almost year-round to include a wide variety of vegetables during the winter, such as tomatoes and zucchini, strawberries in May and lettuce almost every month of the year. Corn and squash abound in the summer months and herbs grow wild.

Soups are also indicative of the regions in which you live. Hearty, stockpot soups are refined to an art form in the Northeast, where a bowl of chowder or hearty stew can be almost medicinal on a biting cold day. Many European favorites are common in the Northeast region of America, as well, including French onion soup that originated in the clear consommé soups from France.

Whether you are preparing chilled soup as a first course on a warm summer day, or a grilled salad on a winter's evening, we invite you to indulge in the easy and delicious results of the recipes in this chapter.

Citrus Zucchini Soup

- 1 medium onion, peeled and thinly sliced
- 1 T. extra virgin olive oil
- 2 medium carrots, peeled and grated
- 3 small zucchini, thinly sliced
- zest from 1 medium orange
- 1 T. curry powder
- 4 c. chicken broth
- juice from 1 medium orange
- 1/2 t. salt
- 1/8 t. ground black pepper
- plain yogurt for garnish
- 8 lemon wedges for garnish

In a large saucepan or stockpot over medium-high heat, cook the thinly sliced onion in olive oil for 3 minutes. Add the grated carrots and cook for 5 additional minutes, stirring occasionally. Add the sliced zucchini and cook until tender. Add the orange zest and the curry powder and stir. Cook for 2 minutes. Add the chicken broth and stir to blend all of the ingredients. Bring to a slow simmer over medium heat. Reduce the heat to low, cover and simmer for 15 minutes. Remove the pan from the heat. Pour the soup into a blender and puree. Return the soup to the saucepan and add the orange juice. Stir well and season with the salt and pepper. Warm through and serve with a dollop of yogurt and a lemon wedge. Makes 8 servings.

Southwestern Chilled Gazpacho

- 1 c. ripe tomato, peeled and finely chopped
- 1/3 c. green pepper, finely chopped
- 1/3 c. celery, finely chopped
- 1/2 c. cucumber, finely chopped
- 1/3 c. onion, finely chopped
- 1 T. fresh parsley, minced
- 1 t chives, chopped
- 1 clove garlic, minced
- 3 T. red wine vinegar
- 2 T. extra virgin olive oil
- 1 t. salt
- 1/4 t. ground black pepper
- 1/2 t. Worcestershire sauce
- 2 c. spicy tomato juice
- sprigs of fresh cilantro for garnish

Combine the tomato, green pepper, celery, cucumber, onion, parsley, chives, garlic, vinegar, olive oil, salt, black pepper, Worcestershire sauce and the spicy tomato juice in a large glass bowl. Chill, covered, for at least 4 hours. To serve, ladle individual servings into refrigerated glass cups or bowls. Garnish each serving with a cilantro sprig. Makes 6 servings.

Icy Cucumber & Green Onion Soup

- 2 1/2 medium cucumbers, peeled
- 4 c. buttermilk
- 1 1/2 T. green onion, chopped
- 1/2 t. salt
- 1/8 t. ground black pepper
- 1/3 c. fresh Italian parsley, finely chopped

Slice 2 of the cucumbers in half and scoop out the seeds. Grate the cucumbers into a bowl. You will have 1 to 1½ cups grated cucumber. In a glass mixing bowl and using a whisk, combine the buttermilk, green onions, salt, pepper and the parsley. Add the grated cucumbers to the mixture and stir thoroughly. Cover and chill for 4 hours. Just before serving, stir the soup again. Ladle the soup into individual chilled bowls and top with thin cucumber slices from the remaining half of the cucumber. Sprinkle with parsley. Makes 8 to 10 servings.

Massachusetts Clam Chowder

- 8 strips bacon, cubed
- 2 T. extra virgin olive oil
- 1 yellow onion, chopped
- 1 large carrot, peeled and chopped
- 2 ribs celery, chopped
- 3 to 4 large potatoes, peeled and diced into 1/2-inch pieces
- 1 1/2 c. bottled clam juice
- 14.5 oz. can diced tomatoes
- 15 oz. can tomato sauce
- 1 t. ground black pepper
- 1 t. seasoned salt
- 1 T. fresh parsley, minced
- 1 T. fresh thyme, minced
- 1 t. fresh marjoram, minced
- 1 t. garlic powder
- 1/2 c. dry white wine
- 13 oz. can minced clams with juice

In a large stockpot, fry the bacon until crispy. Remove the bacon from the stockpot and cool. Crumble the bacon into small pieces. Heat the olive oil in the stockpot over medium-high heat and add the onion, carrot and the celery. Sauté the vegetables until the onions are soft and translucent. Add the potatoes, clam juice, tomatoes, tomato sauce, pepper, salt, parsley, thyme, marjoram, garlic powder and the crumbled bacon. Stir together well and bring to a boil. Reduce the heat to low and simmer until the potatoes are tender, about 25 minutes. Add the wine and clams and return the soup to a boil. Simmer for 5 minutes and serve hot. Makes 6 to 8 servings.

Duo Cheese & White Wine Soup

- 3/4 c. water
- 1/3 c. carrots, shredded
- 1/2 c. celery, chopped
- 1/3 c. white onion, chopped
- 2 T. butter or margarine
- 1/4 c. all-purpose flour
- 1 1/2 c. whole milk
- 1 1/4 c. chicken broth
- 1/2 c. Sauterne
- 1 t. dry mustard
- 1/4 t. ground white pepper
- 1 3/4 c. sharp American cheese, grated
- 1/2 c. cheddar cheese, grated and divided

In a saucepan over medium-high heat, bring the water to a boil. Add the carrots and the celery to the boiling water and cook until tender. Remove from the heat, but do not drain.

In a large saucepan, cook the onion in the butter over medium heat, until transparent. Add the flour and stir until smooth. Slowly add the milk, stirring and cooking until thickened. Slowly add the chicken broth, wine, dry mustard and the white pepper and stir again to blend. Add the American cheese, ¼ cup cheddar cheese and the undrained vegetables. Stir over low heat until the cheese is melted. To serve, ladle the soup into individual bowls and sprinkle the remaining cheddar cheese over the top. Makes 6 servings.

Creamy California Soup with Parmesan Croutons

- 1 T. extra virgin olive oil
- 2 cloves garlic, minced
- 1 medium onion, finely chopped
- 4 c. chicken broth
- 1 1/2 t. ground cumin
- 4 oz. ground almonds
- 1/4 t. ground black pepper
- 1 t. fresh parsley, chopped
- 1/3 c. Parmesan cheese, grated
- 1 oz. flaked almonds
- 4 T. plain yogurt

Preheat the oven to 375°F. Heat the oil in a large saucepan over medium-high heat. Sauté the garlic and onion for 2 to 3 minutes, or until soft and translucent. Add the chicken broth and cumin to the soup. Bring to a boil, reduce the heat to low and simmer. Stir in the ground almonds, black pepper and parsley. If you prefer a smoother consistency, pour the soup into a blender and puree. Reheat the soup in the saucepan after blending and keep warm.

To prepare the croutons, mix together in a

small bowl the Parmesan cheese and flaked almonds. Place 8 even rounds of cheese and almonds on a greased cookie sheet. Cook in the preheated oven for 2 to 3 minutes, until golden. To serve, ladle the hot soup into individual bowls and top each bowl with a Parmesan crouton. Add a dollop of yogurt. Makes 4 servings.

Green Chile & Wild Rice Aztec Chicken Soup

- 1 T. extra virgin olive oil
- 3/4 c. sweet onion, diced
- 1 T. chili powder
- 1 T. orange zest
- 1 t. ground red pepper
- 3 cloves garlic minced
- 2 c. chicken breast, cooked and shredded
- 1/3 c. orange juice
- 6 c. low sodium chicken broth
- 2 c. red bell pepper, chopped
- 1/3 c. carrots, grated
- 1/4 c. seeded green chile, diced,
- 1 T. seeded jalapeño pepper, diced
- 1/2 t. salt
- 3 c. green cabbage, chopped
- 4 c. vegetable juice
- 1 c. uncooked wild rice
- 1 T. chili powder
- 4 plum tomatoes, chopped
- 3 c. canned navy beans, drained
- 1/2 c. sour cream

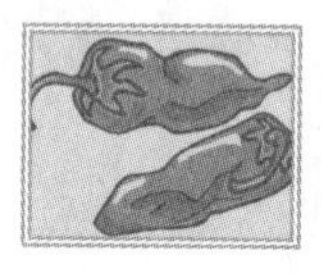

Heat the oil in a large skillet over medium heat. Add the onion, 1 tablespoon of the chili powder, orange zest, red pepper and garlic. Sauté 3 to 4 minutes. Stir in the chicken and the orange juice and cook for 2 minutes, stirring constantly. Add 1½ cups of the chicken broth and bring to a boil. Stir in the bell pepper, carrots, chile, jalapeño and salt. Cook over medium heat 15 minutes. Remove from the heat and set aside.

In a large Dutch oven over medium-high heat, combine the remaining chicken broth, cabbage, vegetable juice, rice, 1 tablespoon of chili powder and the tomatoes. Bring to a boil. Reduce the heat and simmer for 15 minutes. Add the reserved chicken and vegetables and the navy beans and cook for an additional 45 minutes. To serve, ladle the soup into individual bowls and top with dollops of sour cream. Makes 8 servings.

Fireside Potato & Ham Soup

- 3 medium baking potatoes, peeled and cut into quarters
- 1 1/2 c. chicken broth, divided
- 1 1/2 T. unsalted butter
- 1 T. all-purpose flour
- 1 1/4 t. fresh dill, chopped
- 1/4 t. ground black pepper
- 1 c. half and half
- 1/2 c. cooked ham, diced small

Place the potatoes in a large saucepan and cover with water. Bring to a boil and reduce the heat to medium. Cook for 15 to 20 minutes, or until soft. Drain the potatoes. In a blender, combine the potatoes and ¾-cup of chicken broth. Blend until smooth and set aside.

In a medium saucepan over medium-high heat, melt the butter. Whisk in the flour, dill and black pepper until smooth. Add the half and half slowly and cook over low heat until slightly thickened, stirring continuously. Cook an additional minute. Add the potato mixture and the remaining broth. Add the ham and cook and stir over low heat until heated thoroughly. Makes 4 servings.

Linguica Sausage & Hearty Bean Soup

1/2 lb. linguica sausage, sliced
1/4 lb. lean ham, sliced
1 large carrot, grated
1 large potato, diced
1 small onion, chopped
4 c. water
8 oz. can tomato sauce
2 c. macaroni, cooked al dente and drained
1/2 t. salt
15 oz. can kidney beans, drained
1/2 head cabbage, chopped
1 T. fresh parsley, chopped
fresh parsley sprigs

In a large saucepan over medium-high heat, combine the linguica, ham, carrot, potato, onion, water and tomato sauce. Bring to a boil, reduce the heat to low, and simmer for 20 minutes, covered. Add the cooked macaroni, salt, kidney beans, cabbage and parsley. Simmer for an additional 20 minutes. To serve, ladle into individual bowls and garnish with the parsley sprigs. Makes 4 to 6 servings.

East Coast Russian Vegetable Soup

- 1 medium beet, cleaned and cut into chunks
- 1 large carrot, peeled and coarsely chopped
- 1 medium cucumber, coarsely chopped
- 1 medium green bell pepper, seeded and chopped
- 1 small lemon, seeded, peeled and halved
- 1 ripe avocado, peeled, seeded and quartered
- 1/3 c. fresh spinach, packed
- 1/4 c. fresh alfalfa sprouts, packed
- 1/2 c. fresh dill, chopped
- freshly ground black pepper to taste
- 2 c. vegetable broth

In a food processor, blend the beet, carrot, cucumber, bell pepper and lemon until finely chopped. Add the avocado, spinach, alfalfa sprouts, dill and pepper and process again. As the processor is blending, gradually add the vegetable broth and process until smooth. Transfer the soup to a soup tureen or serving bowl, cover and refrigerate until chilled, about 4 hours. Serve in chilled soup bowls and garnish with additional alfalfa sprouts, if desired. Makes 6 servings.

Albondigas Soup

- 1 T. vegetable oil
- 2 T. yellow onion, minced
- 1 clove garlic, minced
- 1 carrot, peeled and thinly sliced
- 1 rib celery, thinly sliced
- 8 oz. can tomato sauce
- 3 c. beef broth
- 1 c. chunky salsa
- 1/2 lb. lean ground beef
- 3 T. soft breadcrumbs
- 2 T. long-grain white rice, uncooked
- 1 egg
- 1 t. salt, divided
- 1/4 t. ground black pepper
- 2 T. fresh cilantro, chopped

In a large saucepan over medium heat, heat the oil and sauté the onion, garlic, carrot and celery until softened. Add the tomato sauce, beef broth and the salsa and stir to combine. Bring the soup to a boil. In a mixing bowl, combine the ground beef, breadcrumbs, rice, egg, ½-teaspoon salt and the pepper. Shape into 18 to 20 meatballs about 1-inch in diameter. Carefully place the meatballs into the simmering soup. Reduce the heat to low, cover and simmer for 25 minutes. Season the soup with the remaining salt and additional black pepper to taste. Ladle into individual bowls and sprinkle cilantro as a garnish. Makes 4 to 6 servings.

Onion Soup Times Four

- 1 T. extra virgin olive oil
- 4 large Vidalia onions, peeled and sliced into 1/4-inch rounds
- 1 bunch scallions, white parts only, sliced into rounds
- 4 large shallots, peeled and chopped
- 2 c. beef broth
- dash salt
- 1/4 t. ground black pepper
- 4 slices French bread, toasted
- 4 slices mozzarella cheese
- 2 T. fresh chives, chopped

In a large skillet over medium heat, heat the olive oil. Add the onions, scallions and the shallots and stir. Reduce the heat to low and cook the onions slowly for 1 hour until they are a golden brown, stirring occasionally. If the onions become too dry, add a little water to prevent burning.

Preheat the broiler. Add the beef broth to the onions and simmer for an additional 15 minutes. Season with the salt and pepper. Ladle the soup into four ovenproof individual bowls. Top each bowl of soup with a slice of toasted French bread and place a slice of mozzarella cheese over each piece of bread. Place the bowls on a sturdy baking sheet and put the bowls 3 inches from the broiler to melt the cheese. Top the melted cheese with a sprinkling of chives. Makes 4 servings.

Sweet Onion & Vine-Ripened Tomato Summer Salad

4 to 5 large, very ripe tomatoes, peeled and cut into wedges

1 small cucumber, peeled and thinly sliced

1/2 Walla Walla or Maui sweet onion, thinly sliced

1 t. fresh dill, snipped

salt and fresh ground black pepper to taste

In a large bowl, combine the tomatoes with sliced cucumber and onion. Add the dill and season generously with the salt and pepper. Toss gently a few times to mix. Cover and let the salad stand for 15 to 30 minutes to allow the flavors to marry. This salad is best when served at room temperature. Do not refrigerate prior to serving. If desired, you may drizzle the salad with a bit of extra virgin olive oil just before serving. Makes 6 to 8 servings.

Other variations: Squeeze one-half of a lemon over the salad before serving to add a fresh tartness. You may add other compatible vegetables, such as avocado, green peppers or zucchini slices. Layer canned sardines across the top of the salad for additional flavor.

Adobe Black Bean, Tomato & Lime Soup

1 T. extra virgin olive oil
1 c. white onion, chopped
1 clove garlic, minced
1/2 c. green bell pepper, chopped
2 t. lime juice
1/2 t. ground cumin
2 t. ground chili powder
1/4 t. ground black pepper
2 c. chicken broth
4 oz. dry spiral pasta
14.5 oz. can diced tomatoes, undrained
2 - 15 oz. cans black beans, undrained
sour cream for garnish

In a large stockpot over medium heat, heat the oil and sauté the onion, garlic and bell pepper until tender. Blend in the lime juice, cumin, chili powder, black pepper and the chicken broth. Bring to a boil. Stir in the pasta and cook 8 to 10 minutes, or until the pasta is cooked al dente. Reduce the heat to low and add the tomatoes and black beans and simmer for an additional 5 to 10 minutes. Ladle the soup into individual bowls to serve and garnish with sour cream. Makes 4 servings.

Tomato, Avocado & Cucumber Salad with Cilantro Dressing

- 2 large ripe avocados, peeled, pitted and diced
- 3 ripe tomatoes, washed and chopped
- 1 cucumber, peeled and chopped
- 1/4 c. green onions, chopped
- 2 dashes hot pepper sauce
- 1 T. fresh lemon juice
- 1 T. fresh lime juice
- 2 T. extra virgin olive oil
- 2 T. fresh cilantro, chopped
- salt and freshly ground black pepper to taste

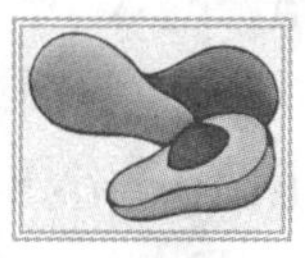

In a salad bowl, gently stir together the avocados, tomatoes, cucumber and green onions. In a small bowl, whisk together the hot pepper sauce, lemon juice, lime juice, olive oil, cilantro, salt and pepper until smooth. Drizzle the cilantro dressing over the vegetables and toss well. Cover tightly and chill for 1 hour to marry the flavors. Makes 4 to 6 servings.

Picnic Red Potato Salad

Salad:

4 lbs large red potatoes

1 T. vegetable oil

8 to 10 hard cooked eggs, peeled and diced

4 green onions, chopped

1 t. seasoning salt

1/4 t. ground black pepper

Dressing:

1 c. mayonnaise

3/4 c. sour cream

2 dashes hot pepper sauce

3 T. prepared hamburger relish

In a large pot of salted water over medium-high heat, bring the red potatoes to a boil. Cook until just tender, approximately 10 to 15 minutes. Do not overcook. Drain the water and allow the potatoes to cool. Peel and cube into 1-inch pieces. Place the potatoes in a large serving bowl. Drizzle the potatoes with the vegetable oil and toss. This will help keep the potato cubes from becoming mushy. Add the eggs and green onions and gently toss again. Add the seasoning salt and ground black pepper and toss again.

In a separate bowl, combine the mayonnaise, sour cream, hot pepper sauce and relish thoroughly. Gently mix the dressing into the potato salad without overmixing. Taste and season the salad again, if necessary. Cover and chill in the refrigerator at least 1 hour, but preferably overnight. Keep chilled prior to serving and refrigerate any leftovers. Makes 10 to 12 servings.

Sweet Spinach Salad with Toasted Almonds & Mandarin Oranges

1/2 c. almonds, slivered or sliced

1 bunch fresh spinach, washed and dried

11 oz. can mandarin oranges, drained and juices reserved

1/2 red onion, sliced paper thin

1 avocado, cut into cubes

Raspberry Vinaigrette:

1/2 c. raspberry vinegar

1/2 c. extra virgin olive oil

2 T. reserved mandarin orange juice

Preheat the oven to 500°F. Place the almonds on a baking sheet and cook in the oven for 3 to 5 minutes. Watch carefully to prevent the almonds from burning. Remove the almonds from the oven and cool on a wire rack. Set aside when cooled.

In a small bowl whisk together the raspberry vinegar, olive oil and mandarin orange juice until blended.

In a large bowl combine the spinach, onion, oranges and avocado. Top the salad with the cooled almonds and drizzle with the vinaigrette. Gently toss. Makes 6 servings.

New Jersey Italian Pasta & Fresh Herb Salad

Herb Dressing:

1/2 c. extra virgin olive oil

1/2 c. red wine vinegar

1/2 t. garlic, minced

2 T. fresh basil, minced

2 T. fresh oregano, minced

3/4 t. ground black pepper

3/4 t. sugar

Pasta Salad:

1 lb. corkscrew pasta, cooked al dente and drained

15 oz. can red kidney beans, drained and rinsed

1/2 cucumber, seeds removed and diced

3 Roma tomatoes, diced

1/2 red onion, diced

6 oz. jar artichoke hearts, chopped

1/2 c. Parmesan cheese, grated

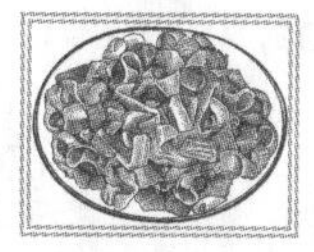

In a large salad bowl, whisk together the olive oil, wine vinegar, garlic, basil, oregano, black pepper and sugar until smooth. Add the cooked pasta, beans, cucumber, tomatoes, onion and artichoke hearts. Toss well to coat the pasta. Cover tightly and chill for at least 2 hours, preferably overnight. Before serving, add the Parmesan cheese and toss to combine. Makes 8 servings.

Summer Ambrosia Fruit Salad

- 1 apple, peeled and chopped
- 2 ripe bananas, peeled and sliced
- 1 fresh peach, peeled, pitted and chopped
- 1 small basket of strawberries, hulled and quartered
- 8 oz. can pineapple chunks, drained
- 1/2 t. ground cinnamon
- 1/2 c. walnuts, chopped
- 1 c. prepared whipping cream

In a large bowl combine the apple, bananas, peaches, strawberries, pineapple and the walnuts. Sprinkle the fruit with the cinnamon and toss. Gently fold in the whipped cream. Serve immediately. Makes 6 servings.

Arugula Salad with Balsamic Vinaigrette

Balsamic Vinaigrette:

1 T. shallots, finely chopped
2 T. balsamic vinegar
1 T. extra virgin olive oil
1/8 t. dried basil
dash salt
freshly ground black pepper

Arugula Salad:

6 c. arugula, washed and torn into bite-size pieces
4 Bartlett pears, cored and chopped
1 T. almonds, chopped
2 t. Romano cheese, grated

In a container with a tight-fitting lid, shake together the shallots, vinegar, olive oil, basil, salt and pepper until blended.

In a salad bowl, combine the arugula and the pears. Drizzle the vinaigrette over the salad and toss to coat. Sprinkle the almonds and the Romano cheese over the top of the salad. Makes 4 to 6 servings.

Cheese Tortellini & Tomato Salad

- 1 lb. frozen cheese tortellini
- 1 c. frozen peas
- 1/2 c. prepared Balsamic Vinaigrette salad dressing
- 8 large Roma tomatoes, washed and cut in rough chunks
- 6 oz. can sliced black olives
- 1 c. mixed salad greens
- 1/2 c. sweet onion, diced
- 1/4 c. pine nuts, chopped

Cook the tortellini according to the package directions. Add the peas during the last minute of cooking just to allow them to thaw. Drain the tortellini and peas and place them in a large salad bowl. Drizzle half of the salad dressing over the pasta and peas and toss gently. Cool. Just before serving, add the tomatoes, olives, greens, onion and the pine nuts. Drizzle the remaining salad dressing over the salad and toss to coat. Serve immediately. Makes 4 to 6 servings.

Roasted Red Pepper & Smoked Turkey Salad

- 1/2 c. smoked turkey, diced
- 1 roasted red pepper, diced
- 4 green onions, chopped
- 1 c. canned kernel corn (you may substitute frozen, thawed corn, if desired)
- 3 T. sour cream
- 1 t. chili powder
- 2 T. lime juice
- 2 T. fresh cilantro, chopped
- 1/4 t. salt
- 1/8 t. ground black pepper
- 1 c. lettuce, torn into bite-size pieces

In a medium bowl, mix together the turkey, red pepper, green onions and corn. In a small bowl, whisk together the sour cream, chili powder, lime juice, cilantro, salt and black pepper until smooth. Drizzle half of the sour cream dressing over the turkey and corn and spoon it into a large salad bowl. Combine the lettuce with the turkey salad and pour the remaining sour cream dressing over all. Toss gently to mix. Makes 2 to 3 servings.

CHAPTER FIVE

Great American Vegetables & Sides

Side dishes and vegetables often provide the transition in a meal, taking it from solid to spectacular. Consider *Wild Rice Pilaf with Dried Cranberries,* and *Artichokes Steamed In White Wine.* Each accompaniment brings life to a simple grilled chicken breast or broiled chop. Even the most unadorned meat is made lively with the delicious choices inside this chapter.

The Northeast region of America offers specialty recipes for vegetables that are heart-warming and nutritious. Recipes such as *Romano Eggplant Marinara, Savory String Beans with Mushrooms & Onions* and *Cilantro & Chives Mashed Red Pototoes* offer inviting goodness for practically any meal. The Southwest region calls for spicy additions to accompaniments that tantalize the tastebuds, such as *Red & Yellow Tomato Pizza, Cayenne Polenta with Wild Mushrooms & Tomatoes* and *Black Beans & Rice with Jalapeño Peppers.*

Mushroom Rice with Italian Parsley

- 6 c. chicken broth or bouillon
- 3 c. long-grain white rice
- 1 T. unsalted butter
- 1 T. extra virgin olive oil
- 1 medium yellow onion, diced
- 8 oz. white button mushrooms, cleaned and sliced
- 1/4 c. Italian parsley, chopped

In a large saucepan over medium-high heat, bring the chicken broth to a boil. Add the rice to the boiling broth. Reduce the heat to low and simmer the rice for 20 minutes, or according to package directions.

In a sauté pan over medium heat, melt together the butter and the olive oil. Add the diced onions and sauté over medium heat for 5 minutes, stirring occasionally. When the onions are translucent, add the sliced mushrooms. Stir through and sauté for another 5 to 10 minutes until the mushrooms are just tender. Stir the mushroom and onions into the prepared rice. Sprinkle with the Italian parsley and serve hot. Makes 10 to 12 servings.

Romano Eggplant Marinara

- 3 medium globe eggplants
- 2 T. extra virgin olive oil
- 1 medium yellow onion, thinly sliced
- 2 cloves garlic, minced
- 2 c. ripe tomatoes, peeled and diced
- 1/2 t. salt
- 1/4 t. ground black pepper
- 1 t. dried oregano
- 1 t. dried basil
- 1/2 c. dry Italian seasoned breadcrumbs
- 1/2 c. Romano cheese, grated

Peel the eggplants and slice into ½ -inch thick slices. Sprinkle the slices with salt and drain in a colander for 30 minutes. Rinse the slices and pat dry with paper towels.

In a large sauté pan over medium-high heat, heat the olive oil and quickly sauté the eggplant, turning once. Drain again on paper towels. Add the sliced onion and the garlic to the skillet and sauté for 5 minutes. Reduce the heat to low, add the tomatoes and cook for 10 minutes, until a sauce forms. Season the tomato sauce with the salt, pepper, oregano and the basil.

Preheat the oven to 400°F. Spoon ⅓ of the tomato sauce into a 5" x 10" baking pan. Place ½ of the eggplant slices on top of the sauce. Spoon a layer of tomato sauce on the eggplant. Place the last layer of eggplant on the sauce. Cover the eggplant with the remaining ⅓ of the sauce. Sprinkle the tomato sauce with the breadcrumbs and the Romano cheese. Bake for 20 minutes. Remove the pan from the oven and let it stand for 15 minutes before serving. Makes 6 servings.

Oven-Roasted Spring Asparagus

1 lb. tender spring asparagus washed, trimmed and cut into thirds.

3 T. extra virgin olive oil

1 T. balsamic vinegar

1 clove garlic, minced

1/4 c. Parmesan cheese, grated

1/4 t. freshly ground black pepper

Preheat the oven to 450°F. In a large bowl, toss the asparagus pieces with the olive oil, balsamic vinegar and minced garlic. Line a baking sheet with aluminum foil and arrange the asparagus pieces in a single layer. Roast the asparagus for 10 to 15 minutes, or until tender. Season with the black pepper to taste. To serve, top with the Parmesan cheese. Makes 3 to 4 servings.

Cilantro & Chives Mashed Red Potatoes

- 3 lbs. red potatoes, washed and quartered
- 3 T. butter
- 1/2 c. buttermilk
- dash hot pepper sauce
- 3 T. fresh chives, chopped
- 1 T. fresh cilantro, chopped
- 1 t. seasoned salt
- 1/4 t. ground black pepper

Place the quartered potatoes in large pan of salted water. Bring the water to a boil over medium-high heat. Slightly reduce the heat and continue cooking at a low boil for 10 to 12 minutes. The potatoes should be tender when pierced with a fork. Drain the water from the potatoes and add the butter. Add the buttermilk, hot pepper sauce, chives, cilantro, seasoned salt and black pepper. Mash the potatoes coarsely and serve. Makes 6 servings.

Savory String Beans with Mushrooms & Onions

- 2 T. butter, divided
- 1 T. extra virgin olive oil
- 1 yellow onion, chopped
- 8 to 12 oz. white button mushrooms, cleaned and sliced
- 1 lb. fresh or frozen, thawed string beans
- 2 t. fresh rosemary, chopped
- 1 t. fresh basil, chopped
- dash dill weed
- 1/2 t. salt
- 1/4 t. ground black pepper

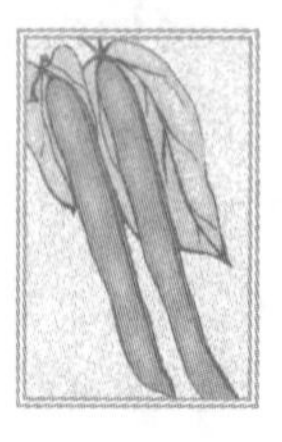

In a sauté pan over medium heat, melt together 1 tablespoon of the butter and the olive oil. Add the onion and sauté for 10 minutes, stirring occasionally Add the sliced mushrooms. Stir through and continue sautéing for another 5 to 10 minutes until the mushrooms are just tender.

Wash and trim the fresh green beans. Place the green beans in a saucepan and add 2 inches of water. Bring the water to a boil over medium-high heat, reduce to medium and cook the beans for 7 to 10 minutes. Drain the green beans into a serving bowl. For frozen green beans, warm them on the stove or in the microwave and then place them in the serving bowl. Add the remaining tablespoon of butter, rosemary, basil, dill weed, salt and black pepper to the warm green beans and stir to blend. Add the mushroom and onion sauté, stir and serve immediately. Makes 4 servings.

Parmesan & Sour Cream Cheese Bake

- 1 lb. corkscrew noodles, cooked al dente and drained
- 3 T. unsalted butter
- 3/4 c. cottage cheese
- 1/3 c. sour cream
- 1/2 c. Parmesan cheese, grated
- 1/2 t. salt
- 1 T. fresh parsley, minced
- Parmesan cheese for garnish

Pour the freshly cooked noodles into a large pasta serving bowl. Stir the butter into the hot noodles. Add the cottage cheese, sour cream and Parmesan cheese, stirring to blend with the noodles. Season with salt and parsley. To serve, sprinkle a garnish of Parmesan cheese over each serving. Makes 6 servings.

Wild Rice Pilaf with Dried Cranberries

- 1 c. wild rice
- 1/2 white onion, quartered
- 1 carrot, peeled and quartered
- 1 rib celery, quartered
- 2 T. extra virgin olive oil
- 2 t. red wine vinegar
- 4 t. shallots, finely chopped
- 2 1/2 T. dried cranberries
- 2 t. orange rind, diced
- 2 T. pine nuts, chopped
- 1 T. fresh Italian parsley, chopped
- 1/4 t. salt
- 1/4 t. ground black pepper

Wash the wild rice in a strainer under cold running water. In a medium saucepan over medium-high heat, place the rice, onion, carrot, celery and enough water to cover. Season with salt and pepper to taste, cover and bring to a boil. Reduce the heat to low and simmer until the rice is tender, about 45 to 60 minutes. Drain the rice and remove the onion, carrot and celery pieces.

In a large bowl, mix together the cooked rice, olive oil, wine vinegar, shallots, dried cranberries, orange rind, pine nuts, parsley and the salt and pepper until well blended. Serve warm or at room temperature. Makes 8 servings.

Shredded Cheese & Broccoli Bake

- 1 medium yellow onion, diced
- 1 clove garlic, minced
- 1 T. extra virgin olive oil
- 3 slices bacon, cooked crisp, drained and crumbled
- 1 head fresh broccoli, broken into florets
- 3 fresh tomatoes, cleaned and chopped
- 2 c. cheddar cheese, shredded
- 6 eggs, beaten
- 1 c. vegetable broth
- 1/4 t. salt
- 1/4 t. ground black pepper
- 1 t. dry mustard
- 1 t. hot pepper sauce

Preheat the oven to 325°F. Grease a 9" x 13" baking pan. In a small skillet over medium heat, sauté the onion and garlic in the olive oil until the onion is translucent. In a large mixing bowl, gently combine the crumbled bacon, broccoli, sautéed onion and garlic, tomatoes, cheddar cheese, beaten eggs, vegetable broth, salt, black pepper, dry mustard and the hot pepper sauce until thoroughly mixed. Pour into the prepared baking pan and bake for 60 minutes. Remove from the heat, cool 10 minutes and serve. Makes 10 to 12 servings.

Red & Yellow Tomato Pizza

1 prepared 12-inch pizza dough
2 to 3 T. extra virgin olive oil
2 cloves garlic, minced
1/2 c. mozzarella cheese, shredded
2 ripe red tomatoes, cleaned and thinly sliced
3 ripe yellow tomatoes, cleaned and thinly sliced
1 T. fresh Italian parsley, chopped
salt to taste
1/4 t. ground black pepper
3 T. Parmesan cheese, grated

Preheat the oven to 450°F. Place the prepared pizza dough on a lightly greased pizza plate or baking sheet. Spread the olive oil on the pizza dough and sprinkle the garlic over the oil. Evenly spread the mozzarella cheese over the dough. Place the tomato rounds on the mozzarella cheese in concentric circles. Sprinkle the tomatoes with the parsley, salt, pepper and Parmesan cheese. Bake for 15 minutes, or until the edges of the crust are lightly browned. Remove the pizza from the oven and let stand for 5 minutes. Slice into wedges. Makes 8 servings.

Skillet Fried Summer Vegetables with Roasted Garlic Dressing

- 1 T. extra virgin olive oil
- 1 red onion, peeled and sliced into 1/3-inch thick rounds
- 1 green bell pepper, cored, seeded and sliced
- 4 oz. fresh button mushrooms, cleaned and thickly sliced
- 1 eggplant, peeled and sliced 1/3-inch thick
- 1 summer squash, peeled and sliced 1/3-inch thick
- 1/2 c. roasted garlic salad dressing
- 1 T. fresh chives, chopped

In a large skillet over medium-high heat, heat the oil. Sauté the onion and green pepper just until the onion becomes limp. Spoon the onion and pepper into a separate bowl. In the hot skillet, sauté the mushrooms for 5 minutes, stirring occasionally. Spoon the mushrooms into the bowl with the onion and green pepper. In the hot skillet, sauté the eggplant and the summer squash until tender, using a spatula to turn the vegetables. Add the bowl of previously sautéed vegetables to the skillet and toss to mix. Add the salad dressing and toss with the vegetables to coat. Spoon the vegetables into a serving bowl and top with the fresh chives. Makes 4 to 5 servings.

Cayenne Polenta with Wild Mushrooms & Tomatoes

Polenta:

1/2 t. extra virgin olive oil

1/4 t. garlic, minced

1 c. whole milk

dash cayenne pepper

1/4 c. yellow cornmeal

1/4 c. Parmesan cheese, grated

salt and pepper to taste

Wild Mushrooms & Tomatoes:

1 T. extra virgin olive oil

1 T. shallots, diced

2 c. shiitake or oyster mushrooms, sliced

8 plum tomatoes, skinned and quartered

1 T. fresh cilantro, chopped

salt and pepper to taste

In a saucepan over low heat, add the olive oil and cook the minced garlic for 1 minute. Add the milk and the cayenne pepper and stir. Increase the heat to bring the milk to a boil. Slowly pour the cornmeal into the hot milk, whisking constantly. After the cornmeal has been added, cook 3 to 4 minutes more, continuing to stir. Remove the pan from the heat and slowly stir in the Parmesan cheese. Season with the salt and pepper to taste. Keep warm.

In a skillet over medium heat, add the oil and cook the shallots until they begin to soften, about 2 minutes. Turn the heat to medium-high, add the mushrooms and sauté another 2 minutes. Add the tomatoes, cilantro and salt and pepper to taste. Remove the skillet from the heat. To serve, place a large spoonful of polenta on a warm plate and spoon the wild mushroom and tomato sauce over the polenta. Serve hot. Makes 4 servings.

Crispy Bacon & Green Onion Potato Bake

1 T. olive oil

4 new potatoes, peeled and thinly sliced

1 T. butter, melted

1/2 t. salt

1/4 t. ground black pepper

2 T. green onions, minced

2 cloves garlic, minced

2 T. bacon bits

4 T. fresh parsley, finely chopped

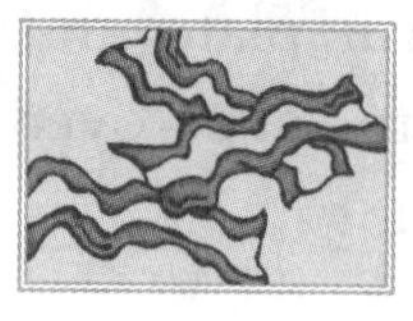

Preheat the oven to 400°F. Using an ovenproof skillet, drizzle the olive oil in the skillet and swirl to coat the bottom and sides of the skillet. Layer half of the potatoes around the pan, beginning in the center and moving out. Sprinkle the potatoes with half of the salt, half of the pepper, green onions, garlic and the bacon bits. Add the remaining potato slices and press down with a large spatula to compress the potatoes. Drizzle with the butter and sprinkle the remaining salt and pepper on top.

Place the skillet on a burner at medium-high heat and cook the potatoes, shaking the pan occasionally, until the potatoes are crisp and brown on the bottom. Remove the skillet from the burner and place it in the oven. Bake for 15 minutes until the potatoes are tender. Remove the skillet from the oven and carefully loosen the edges of the potatoes. Invert the potatoes onto a serving platter. To serve, cut into wedges. Makes 4 servings.

Art's Petite Pea & Parmesan Risotto

- 3 c. chicken broth
- 2 t. olive oil
- 1/3 c. onion, diced
- 1 t. garlic, minced
- 6 oz. bag frozen petite peas
- 1 c. Arborio rice
- 1/4 c. Parmesan cheese, freshly grated
- 1/8 t. ground black pepper
- 1 T. Italian parsley, chopped

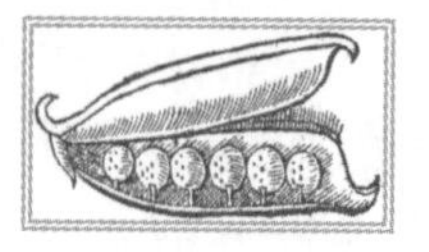

In a saucepan over low heat, heat the chicken broth and keep warm. In a separate saucepan over medium heat, sauté the onion and the garlic in the olive oil until the onion is translucent, about 5 minutes. Add the petite peas and cook and stir for 3 minutes, or until the peas are just thawed.

Add the rice to the onion and peas, stir, and turn the heat to low. Add 1 cup of the hot chicken broth to the rice and stir slowly until the broth is absorbed. Continue adding the broth 1 cup at a time, stirring slowly and allowing the rice to absorb the broth before adding more. The risotto is cooked when it is creamy on the outside and firm in the center. It will take about 20 to 25 minutes to incorporate the broth. Add the Parmesan cheese, the black pepper and the parsley. Stir again to blend. Remove from the heat and serve. Makes 4 servings.

Penne Pasta with Carrots & Sugar Snap Peas

- 1 c. vegetable broth
- 2 lbs. carrots, thickly sliced
- 1/4 lb. fresh sugar snap peas
- 1 lb. penne pasta, cooked al dente and drained
- 1 t. extra virgin olive oil
- 1 T. fresh basil leaves, chopped
- 1/2 t. salt
- 1/4 t. ground black pepper
- 1/2 c. Parmesan cheese, grated

In a large saucepan, bring the vegetable broth to a boil and add the carrots and snap peas. Steam, covered, for 3 to 4 minutes, until the vegetables are just tender. Add the cooked pasta and the olive oil and toss until blended. Add the basil and the salt and pepper and toss again. Spoon the pasta and vegetables into a serving bowl and top with the Parmesan cheese. Makes 4 servings.

Black Beans & Rice with Jalapeño Peppers

1 c. long-grain white rice
1/2 c. onion, chopped
1/4 c. jalapeño peppers, chopped
2 T. butter
2 1/2 c. chicken broth
1/2 t. ground cumin
1 c. canned black beans, rinsed and drained
1/2 c. salsa
2 T. cilantro, chopped

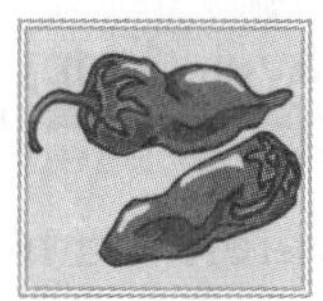

In a saucepan over medium heat, sauté the rice, onion and jalapeño peppers in the butter until the rice turns opaque. Pour the chicken broth and the cumin into the saucepan and bring to a boil. Reduce the heat, cover and simmer until the rice is tender, about 25 minutes. Add the black beans and the salsa and stir. Cook and stir until the beans and rice are heated throughout. Place into a serving bowl and top with the cilantro. Makes 4 servings.

Artichokes Steamed In White Wine

4 large artichokes
1 small onion, finely chopped
1/8 t. dried thyme
1 T. extra virgin olive oil
1 clove garlic, finely chopped
1/8 t. dried basil
2 c. dry white wine
1 t. salt
1/8 t. ground black pepper

Remove any discolored leaves from the artichokes and rinse each artichoke in cold running water. Trim each stem even with the base of the artichoke. Slice 1-inch off the top of each artichoke. Snip off the points of the remaining leaves with scissors. Rinse the artichokes under cold running water again.

In a Dutch oven over medium heat, combine the onion, thyme, oil, garlic and the basil, stirring to blend. Place the artichokes upright in the sauce. Pour the wine over the artichokes. Sprinkle with the salt and pepper. Heat the wine sauce to boiling, cover and reduce the heat to low. Simmer until the bottoms of the artichokes are tender when pierced with a knife, about 30 to 45 minutes.

Carefully remove the artichokes with tongs or 2 large spoons. Place them upright on individual serving plates. Accompany each serving with a small bowl of the wine sauce for dipping. Makes 4 servings.

Deep-Fried Cayenne Pepper Onion Rings

3 large yellow onions
cold water
1 c. all-purpose flour
1 t. salt
1/2 t. cayenne pepper
2 eggs
2/3 c. whole milk
1 T. canola oil
canola oil for deep frying

Peel the onions and cut into ½-inch slices. Separate the slices into individual rings. Place the onion slices into a large bowl and pour the cold water over to cover. Refrigerate for 30 minutes. Drain the onions well in a colander.

Mix together in a medium bowl, the flour, salt and the red pepper. Add the eggs, milk and 1 tablespoon of oil. Beat with a whisk or electric mixer until the batter is very smooth.

Heat the oil to 375°F in the deep fryer. Using tongs, dip a few onion rings into the batter and allow the excess to drip off. Place the onions in the hot oil without overcrowding. Fry until the onion rings are golden brown and turn, about 4 to 5 minutes on each side. Remove the onion rings and drain them on paper towels. Keep the fried onion rings warm, while frying the remaining onion rings. Serve hot. Makes 4 servings.

Tri-Pepper & Tomato Sauté

- 2 T. butter
- 1 T. olive oil
- 1 medium onion, chopped
- 1 c. red bell pepper, chopped
- 1 c. green bell pepper, chopped
- 1 c. yellow bell pepper, chopped
- 2 c. fresh or canned corn kernels
- 4 large ripe tomatoes, chopped
- 1/2 t. salt
- 1/4 t. ground black pepper
- 1 T. Italian parsley, chopped
- 4 slices bacon, cooked crisp and crumbled

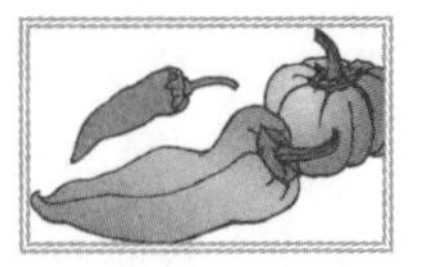

In a large skillet over medium heat, melt the butter and add the olive oil. Sauté the onion until it is soft. Add the bell peppers and the corn and cook for 3 minutes. Add the tomatoes, salt, pepper and the parsley and heat just until warm. Remove the vegetables from the heat and place in a serving bowl. Sprinkle the top of the sautéed vegetables with the crumbled bacon. Makes 6 servings.

Spiced Fall Harvest Vegetables

- 2 1/2 c. winter squash, thinly sliced
- 1 1/2 c. tart baking apples, sliced
- 1/4 c. unsalted butter, melted
- 3 T. dark brown sugar
- 1 t. ground cinnamon
- 1/4 t. ground cloves
- 1/2 c. pecans, coarsely chopped
- 1/4 c. dried cranberries
- 1/2 t. salt
- 1 T. butter, softened

Preheat the oven to 350°F. Lightly spray a 2-quart casserole dish with cooking spray. Place a layer of squash in the dish and cover with a layer of apple. In a small bowl, mix together the butter, brown sugar, cinnamon, cloves, pecans, dried cranberries and salt. Drizzle some of the spices over the apple layer. Continue creating layers of squash and apple with the drizzle of the spice mixture over the top. When the last layer is complete, dot with butter evenly over the top. Cover and bake for 45 to 60 minutes, until the apple and squash are tender and the vegetables are hot throughout. Makes 4 servings.

Sautéed Spinach & Mushrooms

- 2 T. extra virgin olive oil
- 1 medium onion, chopped
- 1 clove garlic, chopped
- 1 lb. white button mushrooms, cleaned and sliced
- 8 oz. jar marinated artichoke hearts with liquid
- 1 lb. fresh spinach, rinsed and dried, in bite-size pieces
- 1/3 c. Parmesan cheese, grated

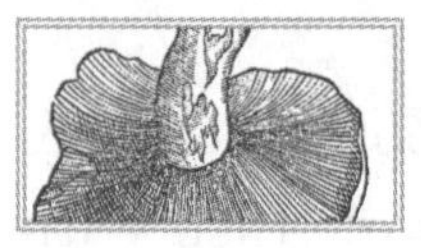

In a large skillet over medium heat, heat the oil. Add the onions and garlic and sauté until the onions are translucent. Add the mushrooms and sauté until they are just tender. Add the artichoke hearts and liquid and stir to combine. Add the spinach, sautéing and stirring until the spinach is heated through. Remove from the heat and spoon the spinach and mushrooms onto a serving platter. Sprinkle the Parmesan cheese over the vegetables and serve hot. Makes 4 servings.

Escabeche (Marinated Vegetable) Salad

- 3/4 c. canola oil
- 1/4 c. white wine
- 2 t. Dijon mustard
- 1 T. fresh oregano, chopped
- 2 t. fresh cilantro, chopped
- 1 t. salt
- 1/2 t. ground black pepper
- 1/2 c. broccoli florets, cooked tender-crisp
- 1/2 c. cauliflower florets, cooked tender-crisp
- 1/2 green bell pepper, cored, seeded and thinly sliced
- 1/2 red bell pepper, cored, seeded and thinly sliced
- 1/2 c. carrots, sliced, cooked tender-crisp
- 1/2 c. yellow onion, thinly sliced
- 1/2 c. red onion, thinly sliced
- 1/2 c. baby corn
- 1 c. pickled jalapeño chiles, drained, sliced and juice reserved

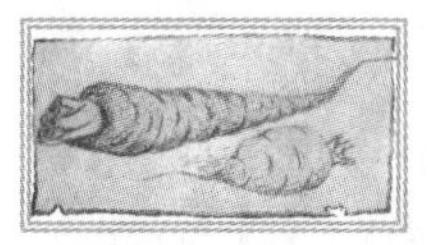

In a blender or food processor, combine the oil, wine, mustard, oregano, cilantro, salt and black pepper and blend at high speed for 5 minutes. In a large glass or plastic mixing bowl, combine together the broccoli, cauliflower, bell peppers, carrots, onions, baby corn and jalapeño chiles. Pour the blended vinaigrette over the vegetables and toss to coat well. Add the reserved jalapeño juice to taste. Toss again. Cover and marinate for at least 2 hours or up to 2 days. Serve chilled. Makes 6 to 8 servings.

CHAPTER SIX

Great American Entrées

The great regions of America call for great entrées and we've provided recipes in this chapter that will highlight the classic choices as well as new, creative combinations that are destined to become favorites!

During the colder months of the year, try such inviting entrées as *Red Wine Beef & Hearty Vegetable Ragoût, New Mexican Tortilla & Salsa Meatloaf* and *Roast Pork Loin with Jalapeño Chutney*. Each will bring warmth and a comfort on a harvest or winter evening. When the days turn warm and fresh produce is in season, include *Salmon Steaks with Shallot & Tomato Relish, Grilled Tequila Chicken Fajitas* and *Chicken Fiesta with Tangy Papaya Sauce*. Each of these recipes will make the most of the season.

Yankee Steamed Clams

3 dozen fresh soft-shell clams
1 c. beer
1 1/2 c. unsalted butter, melted
1 T. fresh parsley, chopped

One hour before serving, scrub the clams with a brush in cold water. Rinse the clams with cold water to rid them of sand. Pour the beer into the bottom of a large stockpot and bring to a boil. Place the clams in a steamer over the beer. Reduce the heat to low, cover the kettle with a tight-fitting lid and steam for 5 to 10 minutes, just until the clams open. Discard any clams that do not open.

To serve, ladle the clams into soup bowls. Place ¼-cup melted butter in a small bowl for each serving. Pour the broth evenly into 4 to 6 mugs and sprinkle each with parsley. To eat, pull the clams from the shells using the neck of the clam. Dip the clam into the broth to swirl away the sand. Next, dip the clam into the melted butter. Eat only the clam body and discard the tough neck. Makes 4 to 6 servings.

Red Wine Beef & Hearty Vegetable Ragoût

- 4 T. extra virgin olive oil
- 1 medium yellow onion, chopped
- 1 clove garlic, minced
- 1 1/2 lb. beef stew meat, cut into 1-inch cubes
- 4 T. red wine vinegar
- 1 c. red wine
- 1 bay leaf
- 1/2 t. dried oregano
- 1/2 c. tomato sauce
- 1/2 t. salt
- 1/4 t. ground black pepper
- 1 T. fresh basil, chopped
- 4 baking potatoes, peeled and cubed
- 2 carrots, peeled and sliced

In a large stockpot over medium-high heat, heat the oil and sauté the onions and garlic until the onions are translucent. Add the meat and sear on all sides. Reduce the heat to medium and add the vinegar, wine, bay leaf, oregano, tomato sauce, salt and black pepper. Reduce the heat to low, cover the stockpot and simmer for 1 hour. Add the fresh basil, potatoes and carrots and simmer for an additional 30 minutes, or until the vegetables are fork-tender. To serve, remove the bay leaf, and ladle the ragoût into large dinner bowls. Makes 4 servings.

Northern Crab & Cheese Manicotti

32 oz. jar marinara sauce
16 oz. ricotta cheese
12 oz. mozzarella cheese, shredded
1 egg
2 T. fresh parsley, chopped
1 T. yellow onion, minced
6 oz. cooked crabmeat, flaked
12 manicotti pasta shells, uncooked

Preheat the oven to 350°F. Lightly spray a 10" x 15" baking pan with cooking spray. Pour half of the marinara sauce into the bottom of the baking pan. Set aside. In a mixing bowl, stir together the ricotta cheese, mozzarella cheese, egg, parsley, onion and crabmeat until combined. Stuff the crab filling evenly into the pasta shells and place the shells in the prepared pan. Pour the remaining half of the marinara sauce over the stuffed pasta shells. Cover the pan tightly with aluminum foil and bake for 30 minutes. Uncover the pan, turn the manicotti, and bake an additional 30 minutes. Remove the pan from the oven and serve hot. Makes 6 servings.

New Mexican Tortilla & Salsa Meatloaf

- 1 1/2 lb. lean ground beef
- 3/4 c. corn tortilla chips, crushed
- 1 egg
- 15 1/2 oz. can whole kernel corn, drained
- 11 oz. jar medium or hot chunky salsa, divided
- 1/2 t. ground cumin
- 1/2 t. ground chili powder
- 1/2 t. salt
- 1/4 t. ground black pepper

Preheat the oven to 375°F. In a large bowl, mix together the ground beef, tortilla chips, egg, corn, 1 cup of salsa, cumin, chili powder, salt and black pepper just until blended. Do not overmix or the meat will toughen. In a small roasting pan, shape the ground beef mixture into a 10" x 5" loaf. Spoon the remaining salsa over the top of the loaf. Bake, uncovered, for 1 hour. Remove from the heat and cool for 10 minutes. Slice thickly and serve. Makes 6 servings.

Vermont Maple Syrup-Glazed Ham

2 T. Dijon mustard
4 T. lemon juice
1 clove garlic, minced
1 t. cracked black pepper
1/4 t. ground nutmeg
1/2 t. ground allspice
1/3 c. Vermont pure maple syrup
3 to 4 lbs. cooked boneless ham

In a small bowl, whisk together the mustard, lemon juice, garlic, black pepper, nutmeg, allspice and the maple syrup to form a smooth glaze. Preheat the oven to 325°F. Place the ham in the roasting pan on a rack. Baste the ham generously with the glaze. Bake for 1 to 1¼ hours, basting with the maple glaze frequently. The ham will be done when a meat thermometer inserted in the thickest part of the ham reaches 140°F. Remove the ham from the oven and let it stand for 10 minutes before slicing. Makes 8 to 10 servings.

Ocean Coast Mussels with Chorizo

- 1 lb. fresh mussels
- 1/2 lb. Chorizo sausage
- 1/2 red bell pepper, seeded and chopped
- 1 clove garlic, minced
- 1 c. white wine
- 2 T. unsalted butter
- 1 T. Italian parsley, chopped
- 1/2 t. dried oregano
- 1/2 t. salt
- 1/4 t. ground black pepper

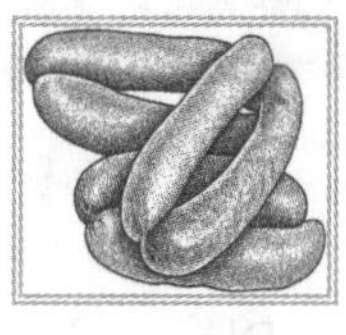

With a brush, scrub the mussels clean and rinse off any sand. In a large skillet over medium-high heat, sauté the chorizo, bell pepper, and the garlic until the garlic is lightly browned. Add the mussels, white wine, butter, parsley, oregano, salt and black pepper and stir to blend. Simmer, covered, over low heat about 5 minutes, or until the mussels open. Discard any mussels that do not open. Remove the skillet from the heat and ladle the mussels into individual bowls to serve. Makes 4 servings.

Roast Pork Loin with Jalapeño Chutney

1 3/4 lbs. pork loin
salt to taste
freshly ground black pepper
2 t. fresh cilantro, chopped
2/3 c. dry white wine

Jalapeño Chutney:
1 c. rice vinegar
1/3 c. dark brown sugar, packed
1/2 c. red bell pepper, diced
1 large jalapeño pepper, seeded and diced
1 T. yellow onion, diced
1 tart apple, peeled, cored and diced
2 t. lemon juice

Preheat the oven to 350°F. Place the pork in a roasting pan and sprinkle with the salt, pepper and the cilantro. Pour the wine into the bottom of the pan. Bake for 1½ hours, basting occasionally with the wine. The pork will be done when a meat thermometer reads 160°F. Remove the pork from the oven and let it stand for 15 minutes, before slicing.

In a medium saucepan over medium-high heat, bring the vinegar and sugar to a boil. Stir until the sugar is dissolved. Add the bell pepper, jalapeño pepper and onion to the pan and continue boiling for 8 minutes. Add the apple, reduce the heat and simmer for 10 minutes, until the apple pieces are tender. Remove from the heat and stir in the lemon juice.

To serve, slice the pork loin and pass the *Jalapeño Chutney* as an accompaniment. Makes 4 servings.

Salmon Steaks with Shallot & Tomato Relish

Salmon:

6 salmon steaks, about 1-inch thick

1 T. extra virgin olive oil

salt to taste

freshly ground black pepper to taste

Shallot & Tomato Relish:

1 T. extra virgin olive oil

1 T. shallots, finely diced

1 t. red bell pepper, diced

1/2 c. fresh tomatoes, chopped

1 1/2 c. corn kernels

1 t. jalapeño pepper, diced

dash ground cumin

1/2 t. sugar

2 T. balsamic vinegar

2 t. fresh cilantro, chopped

dash salt

freshly ground black pepper

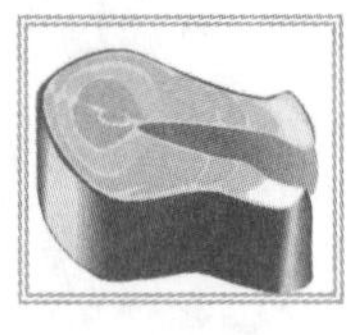

Preheat the broiler. Brush the salmon steaks with the olive oil and season with the salt and pepper. Broil the steaks for 4 to 5 minutes on each side, turning once. The thickness of the salmon steaks will determine the broiling time. The salmon will flake easily when done.

In a skillet over medium heat, heat the oil and sauté the shallots and red bell pepper for 2 to 3 minutes, until soft. Add the tomatoes, corn and jalapeño pepper and cook for 1 minute. Add the cumin and sugar and cook 1 additional minute. Add the vinegar and cook until the liquid reduces slightly. Stir in the cilantro and the salt and pepper to taste.

To serve, evenly divide the *Shallot & Tomato Relish* between 6 warm plates. Place the salmon steaks on top of the relish and serve. Makes 6 servings.

Elegant Seafood-Stuffed Lobster

- 1 1/4 lbs. fresh lobster
- 3 T. unsalted butter
- 2 T. white onion, diced
- 1 t. garlic, minced
- 6 bay scallops, chopped
- 6 medium-size shrimp, peeled, deveined and cut into pieces
- 1/4 c. crab meat, flaked
- 2 c. saltine cracker crumbs

Place the live lobster in fresh water for 15 minutes. This will kill the lobster in a humane fashion. Cut the lobster in half lengthwise, but not all the way through. Remove the intestine (orange material) and discard.

Preheat the oven to 350°F. In a medium skillet, melt the butter and slowly cook the onion and garlic. Add the scallops, shrimp and crabmeat and cook for 2 minutes. Remove the skillet from the heat and stir in the cracker crumbs. Press the stuffing into the length of the lobster. Drizzle with any remaining melted butter. Place the lobster on a cookie sheet and bake for 15 to 20 minutes, until the lobster turns red and the stuffing is golden brown and cooked through. Makes 2 servings.

Grilled Basil & Onion Swordfish

- 1/2 c. extra virgin olive oil
- 1 clove garlic, minced
- 1 T. dry white wine
- 2 t. lime juice
- 1/4 c. fresh basil, chopped
- 1 small onion, diced
- 1/8 t. salt
- 1/4 t. ground black pepper
- 4 - 8 oz. swordfish steaks, about 1-inch thick

Using a resealable plastic bag, combine the olive oil, garlic, white wine, lime juice, fresh basil, onion, salt and black pepper. Add the swordfish steaks, seal the bag and coat the swordfish steaks completely with the marinade. Marinate for 1 hour. Using a grill set on high heat, grill the swordfish for 4 minutes on each side or until firm to the touch. Serves 4.

Chicken Fiesta with Tangy Papaya Sauce

- 8 oz. can tomato sauce
- 1/2 c. orange juice
- 1/2 c. white onion, finely chopped
- 1 T. jalapeño peppers, diced
- 1/2 t. dried oregano
- 1/2 t. chili powder
- 1/4 t. ground cumin
- 1 clove garlic, minced
- 1 T. fresh cilantro, chopped
- 2 dashes hot pepper sauce
- 5 chicken breast halves, boneless, skinless, cut into 1-inch pieces
- 2 t. cornstarch
- 1 T. chicken broth
- 1 c. fresh papaya, chopped
- 3 c. hot cooked rice

In a large skillet over medium heat, combine the tomato sauce, orange juice, onion, jalapeños, oregano, chili powder, cumin, garlic, cilantro and hot pepper sauce. Bring to a boil, stirring occasionally as the ingredients heat. Reduce the heat to low, cover and simmer for 5 minutes.

Add the chicken pieces to the skillet and bring the sauce back to boiling. Cover and simmer for 12 to 15 minutes, until the chicken is tender and no longer pink. In a small bowl, stir together the cornstarch and the chicken broth. Stir into the skillet and cook until thickened and bubbly. Stir and cook 2 additional minutes. Add the papaya and cook just until the papaya is warm. To serve, place the hot rice on a platter and cover with the chicken and papaya sauce. Makes 6 servings.

Old El Paso Chicken

1/4 c. all-purpose flour
1/8 t. ground cumin
salt and ground black pepper to taste
5 chicken breasts, skinless and boneless
4 T. butter, divided
2 poblano chiles, seeded and cut into rings
1/2 yellow onion, peeled and sliced
1/4 c. heavy cream
1/2 c. Jack cheese, shredded

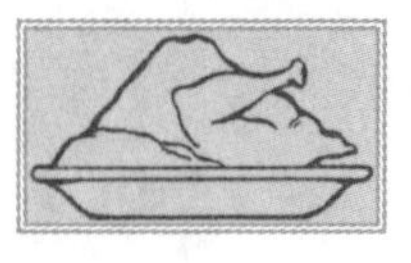

In a small bowl, combine the flour, cumin, salt and pepper and mix well. Cut the chicken breasts into strips. Dredge the chicken strips in the flour and seasonings. In a Dutch oven over medium-high heat, melt 3 tablespoons of the butter. Add the chicken, 5 or 6 strips at a time, and cook 5 to 6 minutes, stirring occasionally. The chicken is done when no pink remains. Remove the chicken from the Dutch oven and keep warm as the remaining chicken is cooked.

Melt the remaining 1 tablespoon of butter in the Dutch oven over medium heat. Add the chiles and the onion and sauté until tender. Gradually stir in the cream. Add the warm chicken and cook until thoroughly heated. Remove the pan from the heat. Sprinkle the cheese over the chicken. Cover just until the cheese melts and serve while hot. Makes 4 servings.

Lobster & Sherry Cream Sauce over Angel Hair Pasta

- 1/4 c. butter
- 1/2 c. onions, diced
- 1 clove garlic, minced
- 2 c. button mushrooms, quartered
- 1 T. all-purpose flour
- 1/4 c. sherry
- 1/2 c. clam juice
- 1 c. cream
- 1 lb. cooked lobster, cut into small pieces
- 1 t. dried marjoram
- 1/2 t. salt
- 1/2 t. ground black pepper
- 1 lb. angel hair pasta, cooked al dente and drained
- 2 T. fresh parsley, chopped

In a large skillet over low heat, melt the butter. Add the onions and garlic and cook for 2 minutes. Add the mushrooms and cook an additional 3 minutes. Stir in the flour completely until no lumps remain and cook for 1 minute. Add the sherry and the clam juice, cooking and stirring until the mixture is thick. Add the cream, lobster, marjoram, salt and the black pepper. Simmer for 10 minutes. To serve, place the pasta on a large serving platter and top with the lobster and cream sauce. Sprinkle the parsley over all to garnish. Makes 4 servings.

Grilled California Flank Steak

1/4 c. fresh orange juice
2 T. chili sauce
2 T. soy sauce
2 T. vegetable oil
1 t. honey
2 cloves garlic, minced
1 t. grated orange rind
2 T. chili powder
1/2 t. salt
1/4 t. ground red pepper
1 1/2 lbs. flank steak, visible fat removed

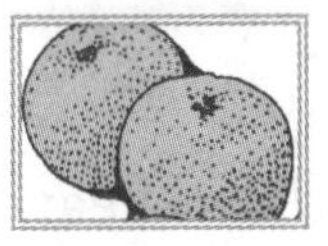

Using a large resealable plastic bag, combine the orange juice, chili sauce, soy sauce, oil, honey, garlic, orange rind, chili powder, salt and red pepper thoroughly. Place the flank steak into the plastic bag and seal. Coat all sides of the meat. Place the meat in the refrigerator and marinate for 8 hours, turning the steak occasionally to coat.

Heat the grill to high heat. Remove the steak from the marinade and discard the marinade. Place the steak on the grill and cook for 4 to 6 minutes on each side, or to your desired degree of doneness. Remove the steak from the grill. Thinly slice the steak on the diagonal across the grain and serve hot. Makes 4 servings.

Enchiladas Olé

- 1 lb. lean ground beef
- 2 c. cheddar cheese, shredded and divided
- 1/4 c. green onions, sliced
- 8 oz. sour cream
- 1 t. dried parsley flakes
- 1/2 t. salt
- 1/8 t. ground black pepper
- 6 oz. can sliced black olives
- 3 - 8 oz. cans tomato sauce
- 1 c. water
- 2 cloves garlic, minced
- 1 t. chili powder
- 1/4 t. dried oregano
- 1/4 t. ground cumin
- 10 soft corn tortillas

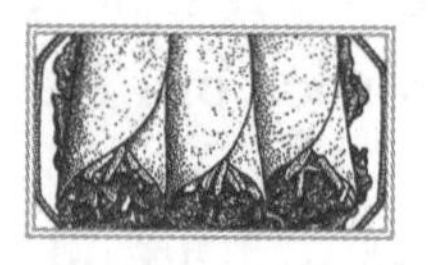

In a large skillet over medium heat, brown the beef until crumbly. Drain off any excess fat. Add ¾-cup cheese, green onions, sour cream, parsley, salt and black pepper, stirring well. Remove from the heat and stir in the olives. Cover and set aside.

In a saucepan over medium heat, combine the tomato sauce, water, garlic, chili powder, oregano and the cumin. Bring to a boil, reduce the heat and simmer for 5 minutes.

Preheat the oven to 350°F. Soften the corn tortillas by wrapping them in a clean dish towel that has been lightly moistened with water. Heat in the microwave for 20 seconds or warm in the oven for 5 minutes. Scoop a tablespoon of the beef mixture into a softened tortilla and roll tightly. Place the filled tortilla, seam-side down, in a 9" x 13" baking pan. Repeat with the remaining tortillas and filling. Pour the enchilada sauce over the filled tortillas and sprinkle with the remaining cheese. Bake, uncovered for 20 to 30 minutes. Serve immediately. Makes 4 to 5 servings.

Citrus Teriyaki Tuna

4 - 6 oz. fresh tuna steaks, about 1-inch thick
1/4 c. soy sauce
1/4 c. mandarin juice
3 strips mandarin zest
3 T. clover honey
dash hot pepper sauce
1 T. fresh cilantro, chopped

In a resealable plastic bag, combine the soy sauce, mandarin juice, mandarin zest, honey, hot pepper sauce and the fresh cilantro until blended. Add the tuna steaks and coat each side with the marinade. Seal and place the steaks in the refrigerator to marinate for 30 to 60 minutes, turning the bag once.

Preheat the grill to high. With a slotted spatula, remove the tuna steaks from the marinade. Strain the marinade into a small saucepan and boil to a thick, syrupy glaze. Grill the fish until cooked to taste, 4 to 6 minutes per side for medium. Brush the tuna steaks with the glaze as they grill. Serve immediately. Makes 4 servings.

MaryAnn's Hawaiian Sweet & Sour Pork

- 2 T. vegetable oil
- 1 clove garlic, minced
- 1 lb. boneless pork, thinly sliced
- 1/2 c. reserved pineapple juice (add water if necessary to make 1/2 cup)
- 1/4 c. vinegar
- 2 T. ketchup
- 2 T. soy sauce
- 1/4 t. crushed red pepper
- 2 T. cornstarch
- 2 T. water
- 15 1/4 oz. pineapple chunks, juices drained and reserved
- 1/2 c. green bell pepper, chopped
- 4 c. hot, steamed rice

In a large skillet over medium-high heat, heat the oil and brown the garlic. Add the pork and stir-fry for 4 minutes. Add the pineapple juice, vinegar, ketchup, soy sauce, cornstarch and water. Stir to mix thoroughly. Reduce the heat and simmer for 10 minutes. Add the pineapple and green pepper and stir again. Simmer on low heat for 4 minutes. To serve, prepare 4 large bowls with individual portions of rice. Spoon the chicken, vegetables and sauce over the rice and serve at once. Makes 4 servings.

Out-West Chuckwagon Beef & Bean Chili

- 1 lb. lean ground beef
- 1 yellow onion, peeled and chopped
- 1 green bell pepper, cored, seeded and chopped
- 2 cloves garlic, minced
- 2 - 14 oz. cans diced tomatoes, undrained
- 14 oz. can red kidney beans, drained
- 14 oz. can chili beans
- 11 oz. can kernel corn, drained
- 8 oz. can tomato sauce
- 1 c. water
- 2 T. chili powder
- 2 t. ground cumin
- 1 t. salt
- 1/4 t. cayenne pepper
- sour cream, shredded cheddar cheese and green onions for garnish

In a Dutch oven over medium-high heat, brown the ground beef. Drain off any excess fat and spoon the meat into a bowl. Set aside.

In the Dutch oven over medium heat, cook the onion and the green pepper until softened. Add the garlic and cook for 1 additional minute. Place the cooked meat, diced tomatoes, kidney beans, chili beans, corn, tomato sauce, water, chili powder, cumin, salt and cayenne pepper in the Dutch oven and mix well to combine. Bring to a boil, reduce the heat to low and simmer for 1 hour. Provide sour cream, shredded cheddar cheese and sliced green onions as garnishes. Makes 6 servings.

Grilled Tequila Chicken Fajitas

- 8 boneless, skinless chicken breasts
- 2 T. extra virgin olive oil
- 2 T. tequila
- 1/4 c. lime juice
- 3/4 t. garlic salt
- 1/4 t. crushed red pepper
- 2 T. extra virgin olive oil
- 1 yellow onion, peeled and thinly sliced
- 1 each red, green and yellow bell pepper, cored, seeded and sliced
- 8 fajita-size flour tortillas
- Sour cream, shredded cheddar cheese, guacamole, salsa and chopped tomatoes for toppings

Place the chicken breasts between 2 pieces of wax paper on a cutting board. Pound the chicken with a mallet to a ¼-inch thickness. In a resealable plastic bag, combine the olive oil, tequila, lime juice, garlic salt and the red pepper thoroughly. Add the chicken breasts, seal the bag and marinate for 1 hour or overnight.

In a skillet over medium-high heat, sauté the peppers and onion in the oil until the vegetables are crisp-tender. Remove from the heat and set aside. Heat the grill to high heat. Remove the chicken from the marinade, discard the marinade, and grill the chicken for 5 minutes on each side. Remove the grilled chicken, slice diagonally and add it to the warm vegetables. To serve, fill the warm tortillas with the fajita chicken and vegetables and add toppings of each diner's choice. Makes 6 servings.

Chicken Fried Steak & Gravy—Texas Style

1 egg
1/4 c. whole milk
1/2 t. salt
1/4 t. ground paprika
1/4 t. ground black pepper
1/4 t. chili powder
4 beef cube steaks
1/4 c. all-purpose flour
vegetable oil for frying

Chicken Fried Steak Gravy:
3 T. all-purpose flour
3/4 c. whole milk
3/4 c. water
salt and black pepper to taste

In a shallow bowl, beat together the egg and the milk. In a small bowl, mix together the salt, paprika, black pepper and the chili powder. Sprinkle the seasonings over both sides of the cube steaks. Dredge the steaks in the flour, shaking off any excess. Dip each cube steak into the egg-milk mixture and then the flour again. Set the steaks aside on a piece of waxed paper.

Using a heavy skillet, pour enough oil into the skillet to a depth of ½-inch. Heat the oil over medium high heat. Carefully place the cube steaks into the hot oil. Reduce the heat and cook 4 to 5 minutes, or until the beef steaks are cooked through. Turn once while cooking. Remove the meat from the pan and drain the steaks on paper towels. Keep warm.

Pour off the oil from the skillet, reserving 2 tablespoons. Place the 2 tablespoons back into the skillet and heat over medium heat. Sprinkle the flour into the hot oil and stir quickly to brown the flour. In a small bowl mix together the milk and water, and gradually add to the hot flour mixture. Constantly stir as the gravy thickens. Reduce the heat as the gravy thickens and add salt and pepper to taste.

To serve, place each fried steak on an individual plate and pour a thin stream of gravy over each. Pass additional gravy at the table. Makes 4 servings.

CHAPTER SEVEN

Great American Desserts

An excellent meal is perfectly complemented by an excellent dessert. The Northeast region of America abounds with inviting choices. Fresh fruit in the summer and the infusion of French and other European cuisine combine to make the desserts decadent and delightful! For a beautiful ending, try *Dreamy Boston Cream Pie, Vermont's Pure Maple Syrup Cake* and *Glazed Maine Wild Blackberry Pie.* For a very special occasion, enjoy *New England Strawberry Decadence Cake* or *Elegant White Chocolate Mousse With Raspberry Sauce.*

Southwestern dessert favorites abound with light flavors and fruit specialties. Inside this chapter you'll find a variety of favorites such as *Bizcochos, Golden Delicious Apple Spice Cake* and *Blackberry Empanandas.*

Sweet treasures of the Mexican culture are found scattered widely throughout cookie and frozen sweets, as well.

Whether you want to prepare any of the recipes in this chapter for an elegant dessert or informal sweet snack, we hope that you'll find a little bit of the taste of both the Northeast and the Southwest in these choices.

Double Chocolate After School Cookies

1 c. butter, softened
1 1/4 c. sugar
2 eggs
2 t. vanilla extract
2 c. all-purpose flour
2/3 c. baking cocoa
3/4 t. baking soda
1/4 t. salt
2 c. semi-sweet chocolate chips

Preheat the oven to 350°F. In large mixing bowl, beat together the butter, sugar, eggs and vanilla until light and fluffy. In a separate bowl, stir together the flour, cocoa, baking soda and salt. Add the flour mixture to the creamed mixture and mix well. Stir in the chocolate chips. Drop by rounded teaspoonfuls onto an ungreased cookie sheet. Bake 8 to 10 minutes. Let the cookies cool on the cookie sheet, and then place them on a wire rack to finish cooling. Store in an airtight container. Makes about 4½ dozen cookies.

Hawaiian Macadamia & Chocolate Chip Cookies

2 1/2 c. rolled oats, regular or quick-cooking

1 c. butter, softened

1 c. dark brown sugar, packed

1 c. sugar

2 eggs

2 c. all-purpose flour

1/2 t. salt

1 t. baking powder

1 t. baking soda

12 oz. pkg. semi-sweet chocolate chips

8 oz. sweet chocolate bar, chopped

1 t. vanilla extract

1 1/2 c. macadamia nuts, finely chopped

Preheat the oven to 375°F. Measure the oats into a blender or food processor and process until the oats are a fine powder. Set aside. In a large mixing bowl, cream together the butter and both sugars until fluffy. Add the eggs and vanilla and blend well. Mix in the oatmeal powder, the flour, salt, baking powder and baking soda. Add the chocolate chips, chopped chocolate bar, vanilla and the macadamia nuts. Mix well until all ingredients are incorporated. Roll the dough into balls the size of small golf balls and place the balls 2 inches apart on an ungreased cookie sheet. Bake for 10 minutes. Remove the cookies to a wire rack to cool. Makes 4 dozen cookies.

Dreamy Boston Cream Pie

Cake:
7 eggs, separated
1 1/4 c. sugar, divided
1 c. all-purpose flour
2 T. butter, melted

Pastry Cream:
1 T. butter
2 c. whole milk
2 c. light cream
1/2 c. sugar
3 1/2 T. cornstarch
6 eggs
1 t. dark rum

Icing:
6 oz. semisweet chocolate
1/4 c. water
toasted almond slivers for garnish

Preheat the oven to 350°F. Grease a 10-inch round cake pan. In a large mixing bowl, beat the egg yolks and ¾-cup sugar until smooth and creamy. In a separate large mixing bowl, beat the egg whites with ½-cup sugar until the whites form peaks. Fold the egg whites into the yolk mixture. Gradually add the flour, mixing with a spatula. Mix in the butter. Pour the batter into the prepared pan and bake for 20 minutes, or until the cake is spongy and golden. Remove from the oven and cool for 5 minutes on a wire rack. Invert the cake to the wire rack and cool completely.

In a saucepan over medium heat, combine the butter, milk and cream and bring it just below a boil. In a separate bowl, whisk the sugar, cornstarch and the eggs together until ribbons form. Slowly whisk this mixture into the hot cream mixture and cook to a boil, stirring constantly. Boil for 1 minute. Pour the pastry cream into a bowl and cover the surface with plastic wrap. Chill 4 hours or overnight. When the pastry cream is chilled, add the rum and whisk again to smooth. Set aside.

Cut the sponge cake in half horizontally to make two layers. Place one layer on a serving platter. Spread the chilled pastry cream over one layer, reserving enough to frost the cake sides. Top with the second cake layer. Melt the semisweet chocolate in a small saucepan, and thin to the desired consistency with warm water. Spread the thin layer of chocolate icing over the top layer of cake. Sprinkle with the slivered almonds. Frost the sides of the layers with remaining pastry cream. Chill the cake before serving and keep any leftover cake refrigerated. Makes 10 to 12 servings.

Bizcochos

- 1 c. shortening
- 1/3 c. sugar
- 1/3 c. white wine
- 2 egg yolks
- 3 c. all-purpose flour
- pinch salt
- 1/2 t. ground cinnamon
- powdered sugar for dusting

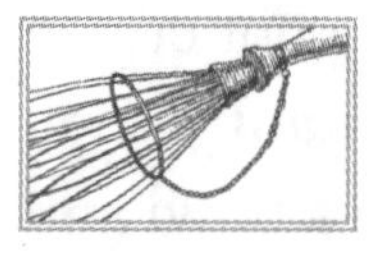

Preheat the oven to 375°F. In a mixing bowl, cream together the shortening, sugar and the wine. Add the egg yolks one at a time, beating after each addition. In a separate bowl, combine the flour, salt and the cinnamon. Add the flour mixture to the shortening mixture and blend thoroughly. On a lightly floured board, roll the dough to ⅛-inch thickness. Cut the cookie dough into diamond shapes. Place the diamond shapes on an ungreased cookie sheet and bake for 6 to 8 minutes. Remove the cookies from the oven and sprinkle them with the powdered sugar. Store loosely wrapped. Makes 3 dozen cookies.

Blackberry Empanandas

2 c. all-purpose flour	1 T. whole anise seed
2 t. baking powder	1/2 c. shortening
3/4 t. salt	5 to 7 T. ice water
3/4 c. sugar	16 oz. can blackberry pie filling

Preheat the oven to 350°F. In a medium bowl, combine the flour, baking powder, salt, sugar and the anise. With a pastry blender, cut in the shortening until the mixture is crumbly. Sprinkle with the ice water and stir with a fork until the pastry holds together. Divide the pastry evenly into 18 small balls. On a lightly floured piece of wax paper, roll each piece into a 4-inch round. Place 2 tablespoons of blackberry pie filling on one-half of each round. Fold the other half over the filling. Press the edges together with the tines of a fork to seal. Arrange the empanadas on a cookie sheet and prick the tops of each 3 or 4 times with a fork. Bake for 30 minutes. Remove the empanadas from the oven and place on a wire rack to cool. Serve hot or cold. Makes about 1½ dozen.

Milk Chocolate Crumb Bars

- 3/4 c. butter, softened
- 2 c. all purpose flour
- 1/2 c. granulated sugar
- 1/4 t. salt
- 1 3/4 c. semi-sweet chocolate chips, divided
- 1 1/4 c. sweetened condensed milk
- 1 t. vanilla extract
- 1 c. walnuts, chopped (optional)

Preheat the oven to 350°F. Grease a 9" x 13" baking pan. In a large mixing bowl, beat the butter until creamy. Beat in the flour, sugar and salt until crumbly. Press 2 cups of the crumb mixture onto the bottom of the prepared baking pan, reserving the remaining mixture. Bake the crumb crust for 10 to 12 minutes, or until the edges are golden. Place the baking pan on a wire rack.

Warm 1 cup of the chocolate chips together with the sweetened condensed milk in a small, heavy saucepan over low heat. Stir until smooth. Stir in the vanilla. Spread the chocolate filling over the hot crust. In a small bowl, stir together the walnuts and the remaining chips into the reserved crumbs. Sprinkle the topping over the chocolate filling. Bake for another 25 to 30 minutes, or until the center is set. Remove from the oven and cool completely on a wire rack. Makes 15 to 18 bars.

Vermont's Pure Maple Syrup Cake

- 2 1/2 c. all-purpose flour
- 2 t. baking powder
- 2 t. baking soda
- 1/2 t. salt
- 1 t. ground cinnamon
- 1/2 c. butter, softened
- 1/2 c. sugar
- 2 large eggs
- 1 c. Vermont pure maple syrup
- 2 t. vanilla extract
- 1/2 c. water

Frosting:

- 2 c. powdered sugar
- 1/4 t. vanilla extract
- 4 T. Vermont pure maple syrup
- 2 to 3 T. milk for desired consistency

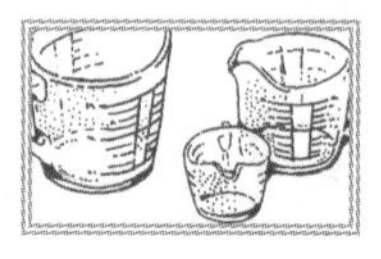

Preheat the oven to 350°F. Lightly spray two 9-inch cake pans with cooking spray. Dust each with flour and shake out any excess. Set aside. In a medium bowl, sift together the flour, baking powder, baking soda, salt and the cinnamon. In a large bowl, using a mixer on high speed, beat the butter and sugar until light and fluffy. Add the eggs, one at a time, beating after each addition. Add 1 cup of the maple syrup and the vanilla and mix. Reduce the mixer speed to low. Add the dry ingredients by thirds, alternating with the water, and ending with the flour mixture. Pour the batter evenly into the prepared cake pans. Bake for 30 minutes. A toothpick inserted in the center of each cake will come out clean when the cake layers are done. Remove the cakes from the oven and cool on a wire rack for 10 minutes. Invert the cakes onto the wire racks to finish cooling.

In a medium bowl, mix together the powdered sugar, vanilla and the maple syrup until smooth. Add enough milk to reach your desired consistency.

When the cakes are completely cooled, place one cake layer on a serving platter. Spread the frosting over the top of the layer. Place the second cake layer on top of the first one. Frost the top and sides of the cakes. Makes 8 to 10 servings.

Pumpkin & Spice Cheesecake

2 c. cream cheese, softened
1/2 c. sugar
1 t. vanilla extract
2 eggs
1/2 c. canned pumpkin puree
1/2 t. ground cinnamon
dash ground cloves
dash ground nutmeg
1 prepared graham cracker crust (9-inch)

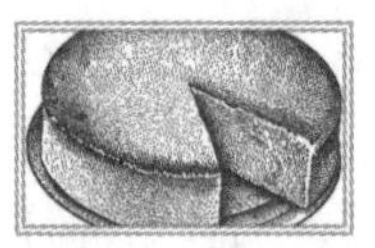

Preheat the oven to 350°F. In a mixing bowl, beat the cream cheese, sugar and the vanilla and mix until well blended. Add the eggs to the cream cheese mixture and stir together until creamy. Spoon 1 cup of the cream cheese mixture into a medium mixing bowl. Add the pumpkin, cinnamon, cloves and nutmeg and stir well. Pour the plain cheesecake batter into the crust. Top with the pumpkin batter. Bake for 35 to 40 minutes, until the center is almost set. Remove the cheesecake from the oven and let it cool on a wire rack. Chill for 3 hours or overnight and serve. Refrigerate any leftovers. Makes 8 servings.

Warm Spiced Apple & Orange Crisp

- 4 c. tart apples, peeled, cored and sliced
- 1/4 c. orange juice
- 1 t. orange zest
- 1 c. sugar
- 1 c. all-purpose flour
- 1 t. ground cinnamon
- 1/4 t. ground nutmeg
- dash salt
- 1/2 c. unsalted butter

Preheat the oven to 375°F. Spread the sliced apples in a buttered 9-inch pie plate. Sprinkle orange juice over the top of the apples and then top with the orange zest. In a medium bowl, combine the sugar, flour, cinnamon, nutmeg and a dash of salt. Cut in the butter with a pastry blender until the mixture is crumbly. Scatter the pastry evenly over the apples. Bake for 45 minutes, or until the apples are soft and the topping is crisp. Remove from the oven and serve warm with ice cream. Makes 6 servings.

Fresh Bartlett Pear Cobbler

1 1/2 T. cornstarch
1/3 c. dark brown sugar, packed
1/2 c. cold water
4 c. fresh Bartlett pears, cored, sliced and sprinkled with sugar
1 T. unsalted butter
1 1/2 T. fresh lemon juice

Topping:
1 c. flour
1 T. sugar
1 1/2 t. baking powder
1/4 t. salt
1/4 c. cold butter
1/4 c. whole milk
1 egg, slightly beaten
granulated sugar

Preheat the oven to 400°F. In a saucepan over medium heat, mix together the cornstarch, brown sugar and the water. Add the pears and cook, stirring, until the pears have softened and the sauce has become slightly thick. Stir in the butter and the lemon juice and mix well. Pour the pears and sauce into an 8-inch round baking dish. Set aside.

In a medium bowl, mix together the flour, sugar, baking powder and the salt. With a pastry cutter, cut in the cold butter until the mixture resembles coarse crumbs. Mix in the milk and the egg and stir just until the dry ingredients are moistened. Drop by spoonfuls onto the hot pear filling. Sprinkle the top evenly with granulated sugar. Bake for 20 minutes, or until the topping is golden brown. Remove from the oven, cool slightly on a wire rack, and serve warm. Makes 6 servings.

Tangy Lemon Pudding Bars with A Pecan Crust

Crust & Topping:
8 oz. pkg. lemon cake mix
1/2 c. unsalted butter
1/2 c. pecans, chopped

Filling:
4 oz. pkg. lemon pudding and pie filling (not instant)
12 oz. can sweetened condensed milk
2 T. fresh lemon juice
2 t. lemon extract

Glaze:
1 1/2 c. powdered sugar
1 T. lemon extract
1 T. butter, softened
2 t. whole milk

Preheat the oven to 350°F. In a mixing bowl, cut together the cake mix, butter and pecans until the mixture is pea-sized. Reserve 1 cup for the topping. Press the crust firmly into a 9" x 13" baking pan.

In a separate bowl, mix the lemon pudding mix, condensed milk, lemon juice and the lemon extract until smooth and creamy. Pour the lemon filling evenly over the prepared crust. Sprinkle with the reserved topping. Bake for 25 minutes. Remove the pan from the oven and allow it to cool for 10 minutes on a wire rack.

In a small bowl, mix together the powdered sugar, lemon extract, butter and milk until smooth. Add just enough milk for the desired consistency. Drizzle the glaze over the top of the warm bars. Cool 20 minutes, then cut and serve. Makes 20 to 24 bars.

Rich Mocha Nut Torte

Crust:

1 1/4 c. almonds, blanched

3 T. sugar

3 1/2 T. cake flour

6 T. unsalted butter, cut into small pieces

Filling:

2 eggs

1 egg yolk

1 1/4 c. dark brown sugar, packed

1/2 c. cold coffee

1 c. all purpose flour

1/2 c. cocoa powder

1 t. baking powder

1 c. hazelnuts, coarsely chopped

3/4 c. walnuts, coarsely chopped

1 c. powdered sugar

prepared whipping cream

Preheat the oven to 350°F. In a food processor, grind the almonds with the granulated sugar. Add the flour and process to blend. Add the butter and turn the machine quickly on and off until the mixture resembles coarse meal, or cut in by hand with a pastry cutter. Press the almond-butter crust into the bottom and up the sides one-third of the way in an ungreased 9-inch springform pan. Set aside.

In a mixer bowl, beat with an electric mixer the whole eggs, egg yolk, brown sugar and coffee until fluffy, 4 to 5 minutes. In a separate bowl, sift and mix the flour, cocoa powder and baking powder together. Gently fold the flour mixture into the egg-sugar mixture. Fold in the hazelnuts and walnuts. Do not over mix. Pour the filling into the prepared crust. Bake in the center of the oven for about 40 minutes. The torte filling will be soft in the center and dry 1-inch from the edge when tested.

Remove the pan from the oven and allow the torte to cool in the pan on a wire rack. Run a sharp knife around the edge of the cake pan and the torte crust. Release the spring on the form and place the torte on a serving platter. Dust with powdered sugar and serve with whipped cream. Makes 8 to 10 servings.

Glazed Maine Wild Blackberry Pie

Crust:

2 c. shortbread cookies, crushed

1/4 t. ground cinnamon

1/2 c. unsalted butter, melted

Filling:

4 c. wild blackerries, rinsed and drained

3/4 c. + 2 T. sugar

3 T. cornstarch

dash lemon juice

1 c. prepared whipped cream for garnish

In a small bowl, mix together the crushed cookies and cinnamon. Add the butter and mix until crumbly. Press the crust into a 9-inch pie pan. Set aside.

In a medium bowl, sprinkle 2 cups of the berries with 2 tablespoons sugar and set aside. Place the remaining blackberries in a saucepan over medium heat. Add ¾-cup sugar and mash the berries. Stir until the sugar begins to dissolve. Add the cornstarch to the mashed berries and cook over medium heat until the berries are soft and the sauce is thickened and clear. Cool slightly and add the lemon juice.

Pour the uncooked reserved berries into the prepared pie crust. Pour the cooked berry filling over the berries. Cover and chill 4 to 6 hours, or until set. To serve, place a wedge of pie on individual plates and garnish with the whipped cream. Makes 8 servings.

Elegant White Chocolate Mousse With Raspberry Sauce

1 lb. white chocolate, melted
8 oz. cream cheese, softened
1/2 t. vanilla extract
1 qt. prepared whipped cream

Raspberry Sauce:
2 c. fresh raspberries
5 T. powdered sugar

In a mixing bowl, combine the chocolate, cream cheese and vanilla until smooth. Fold in the whipping cream and refrigerate for 1 hour. Whip the chilled chocolate cream again. Spoon the chocolate mixture into serving glasses and return to refrigerator for 1 to 2 hours until set.

In a small saucepan over low heat, combine the raspberries and the sugar. Cook and stir until the berries are soft, 3 to 4 minutes. Pour the raspberries into a food processor and puree. Strain the raspberry puree through a sieve and discard the seeds. Let the raspberry sauce stand to cool. To thin the sauce to your desired consistancy, add 1 tablespoon of cold water at a time, stirring after each addition. To serve, drizzle the raspberry sauce over each glass of white chocolate mousse. Makes 8 to 10 servings.

Chocolate Fudge in Chocolate Cake

2 1/2 c. all-purpose flour	1 2/3 c. sugar
3/4 c. unsweetened cocoa	1 t. vanilla extract
1 t. baking soda	1 c. mayonnaise
1 t. baking powder	1 1/3 c. water
1/2 t. ground cinnamon	chocolate fudge syrup
3 eggs	1 1/2 c. powdered sugar

Preheat the oven to 375°F. Grease and flour a 9" x 13" baking pan. Sift together the flour, cocoa, baking soda, baking powder and the cinnamon. In a separate bowl, mix together the eggs, sugar, vanilla and the mayonnaise. Using an electric mixer at high speed, beat the batter for 3 minutes. Alternately add the dry ingredients and the water into the batter, blending as each addition is made. Mix thoroughly. Pour the batter into the pan and bake 35 to 40 minutes. The cake will spring back when touched lightly. Remove the cake from the oven and place it on a wire rack. Using a toothpick, poke holes into the cake 1-inch apart all over the top of each cake. Drizzle the chocolate fudge syrup into the holes and over the top of the cake. Allow the cake to cool and dust with the powdered sugar. Makes 12 to 15 servings.

Texas Red Velvet Cake

1/2 c. butter, softened
1 1/2 c. sugar
2 eggs
1 1/2 t. vanilla extract
1 1/2 oz. bottle red food coloring
2 1/2 c. cake flour, sifted
1 t. salt
1 t. baking powder
1 1/4 c. cocoa
1 c. buttermilk
1 t. baking soda
1 T. cider vinegar

Frosting:

2 - 3 oz. pkgs. cream cheese, softened
6 T. butter, softened
1 t. vanilla extract
2 c. powered sugar, sifted

Preheat the oven to 350°F. Grease and flour two 9-inch cake pans. In a mixing bowl, cream together the butter, sugar, eggs, vanilla and the red food coloring. Set aside.

In a separate bowl, sift together the flour, salt, baking powder and the cocoa. Alternately add the dry ingredients and the buttermilk into the creamed butter and sugar, ending with the dry ingredients. In a small bowl mix together the baking soda and vinegar. Stir into the batter without overmixing. Evenly pour the cake batter into the two cake pans and bake for 25 to 35 minutes, or until done. A toothpick inserted in the center of the cakes will come out clean when the cakes are done. Remove the cakes from the oven and cool completely on wire racks.

In a mixing bowl, cream together the cream cheese, butter and the vanilla until smooth. Add the powdered sugar in stages, until the frosting reaches a good spreading consistency. Place one cake layer on a serving platter. Cover the layer with frosting. Place the second layer on top of the frosted layer. Frost the top and the sides of the double layers. To serve, cut into wedges. Makes 8 to 10 servings.

Old-Fashioned Oatmeal Cranberry Cookies

1/2 c. shortening	1 t. salt
1 1/4 c. sugar	1 t. ground cinnamon
2 eggs	1/4 t. ground cloves
6 T. dark molasses	2 c. rolled oats, regular-style
1 3/4 c. all-purpose flour	1/2 c. walnuts, chopped
1 t. baking soda	1 c. dried cranberries

Preheat the oven to 400°F. In a large mixing bowl, cream together the shortening, sugar, eggs and the molasses. In a separate bowl, sift together the flour, soda, salt, cinnamon and cloves. Add the dry ingredients to the creamed mixture and blend well. Stir in the oatmeal, walnuts and dried cranberries.

Drop by spoonfuls onto an ungreased cookie sheet. Bake for 8 to 10 minutes, or until cookies just start to brown. Remove from the oven to a wire rack to cool. Store the cooled cookies in an airtight container. Makes 3 dozen.

Golden Delicious Apple Spice Cake

- 2 c. sugar
- 1/2 c. vegetable oil
- 2 eggs
- 4 c. Golden Delicious apples, peeled cored and diced
- 2 1/4 c. all-purpose flour
- 1 t. salt
- 2 t. ground cinnamon
- 3/4 t. ground nutmeg
- 2 t. baking soda
- vanilla ice cream, whipped cream and/or caramel sauce

Preheat the oven to 325°. In a large mixing bowl, combine the sugar, oil and eggs. Mix in the apples and blend well to combine. Sift together the flour, salt, cinnamon, nutmeg and soda and add to the apple batter. Thoroughly mix and pour into a greased and floured 9" tube or bundt pan. Bake for 1 hour or until a toothpick inserted in the center comes out clean. Cool slightly and serve warm with vanilla ice cream, whipped cream and caramel sauce. Serves 8.

New England Strawberry Decadence Cake

Cake:
3 c. cake flour
1/2 t. baking soda
1/2 t. salt
1 c. unsalted butter, softened
2 c. sugar
3 large eggs, at room temperature, beaten lightly
1 t. strawberry flavoring
1 t. vanilla extract
1 c. buttermilk, at room temperature

Syrup:
2 c. strawberries, mashed
1/4 c. sugar

Filling:
1 1/2 c. strawberry jam

Frosting:
1 c. heavy cream
3 1/2 T. sugar
1 c. sour cream

Preheat the oven to 325°F. Butter two 9-inch cake pans and line each with parchment or waxed paper. Butter and flour the parchment paper. In a medium bowl, sift together the flour, baking soda and salt and set aside. In a separate bowl, beat the butter and add the sugar, a little at a time until light and fluffy. Beat in the eggs, strawberry flavoring and the vanilla. Beat in ⅓ of the sifted dry ingredients alternately with ½ of the buttermilk, mixing well. Repeat the process, ending with the dry ingredients and mix until smooth. Pour the batter evenly into the prepared pans and bake for 45 minutes, or until a toothpick inserted in the center of the cakes comes out clean. Transfer the cakes to wire racks and cool in the pans for 20 minutes.

While the cake is cooling, in a small saucepan over medium heat, stir together the strawberries and sugar until the sugar is dissolved. Heat and cook over medium heat for 5 to 7 minutes. Pour the sauce through a sieve and discard the seeds. With a toothpick, poke holes at ½-inch intervals in the cooling cake layers. Spoon the syrup over each layer, allowing the syrup to be completely absorbed before adding more syrup. Allow the cake layers to cool completely.

In a bowl, whisk the heavy cream with the sugar until it forms firm peaks. Add the sour cream, a little at a time, and whisk until it is of spreading consistency.

To assemble the cake, place 1 cake layer on a cake plate or serving platter and carefully peel off the waxed paper. Spread ⅔ of the strawberry jam over the top. Invert the second cake layer onto the top of the first layer and peel off the waxed paper.

Spoon the remaining jam onto the center of the layer, leaving a 1½-inch border around the edge. Frost the cake with the sour cream frosting around the border of the jam, leaving the jam exposed, and frost the sides of the cake. Frost the top of the cake with the sour cream frosting and chill the cake for at least 2 hours before serving. Refrigerate any leftovers. Makes 8 to 10 servings.

Dutch-Inspired Shoofly Pie

1 unbaked 9-inch pie shell

Filling:
1 t. baking soda
1 c. boiling water
2/3 c. light corn syrup
1/3 c. dark molasses

Crumb Topping:
1 c. all-purpose flour
1/4 c. vegetable shortening
1/2 c. light brown sugar

In a medium bowl, dissolve the baking soda in the boiling water. Add the corn syrup and the molasses. Stir well. Pour this into the unbaked pie shell.

In a medium bowl, combine the flour, shortening and the brown sugar with a pastry cutter until it resembles coarse crumbs. Sprinkle this evenly over the top of the filling. Bake for 10 minutes, then reduce the heat to 350°F. Continue baking for another 25 minutes. The pie should be set, but not dry. Be careful to not overbake. Remove the pie from the oven, place on a wire rack to cool and then serve. Serves 8.

Praline Pecan Tarts

Crust:

1 c. butter, softened

2 3-oz. pkg. cream cheese, softened

2 c. flour

Filling:

2 eggs

2 T. butter, melted

1/2 t. vanilla extract

1 1/2 c. brown sugar, firmly packed

1 c. chopped pecans

Preheat the oven to 350°F. In a medium bowl, cream together the butter, cream cheese and the flour using a pastry blender or two knives. Blend well. Form the dough into 1-inch diameter balls. Press the balls into the cups of miniature muffin tins. This forms the crust for the filling.

In a medium bowl, combine the eggs, melted butter, vanilla and the brown sugar blending well. Stir in the chopped pecans. Place a teaspoonful of this mixture into the uncooked crusts in the muffin tins. Bake for 20 to 30 minutes, checking on doneness. The tarts will be finished when the filling is set. Remove the pans from the oven and cool on wire racks. Slide a knife around the edge of each tart. When the tarts are cool, remove them from the muffin tins and cool completely on wire racks. Makes about 48 mini tarts.

South of the Border Coconut Flan

7 egg yolks
6 T. sugar, divided
Pinch of salt
2 c. half and half
1/2 c. cream of coconut
2 t. vanilla extract
1/2 c. + 2 T. shredded coconut

Preheat the oven to 350°F. In a large bowl, mix the egg yolks and 3 tablespoons of the sugar along with the pinch of salt. Mix until well-blended, about 2 minutes. In a medium saucepan over low heat, heat the half and half, cream of coconut, vanilla, the remaining 3 tablespoons of sugar and the shredded coconut, stirring constantly. Bring the mixture just to boiling and wait 30 seconds longer. Remove the pan from the heat and stir this creamy mixture once or twice. Add this to the egg yolk mixture, stirring to blend well.

Place 8 6-oz. ramekins in a baking pan. Pour the coconut mixture evenly into the ramekins. Add water to the baking pan until the level of water reaches ⅔ of the way up the sides of the ramekins. Bake the flans for 50 minutes. Remove the ramekins from the heat and place them on wire racks to cool. When they are cool enough to touch, place them in the refrigerator and chill for several hours. Serves 8.

Manhattan White Chocolate Nut Torte

1/4 c. graham cracker crumbs
1 lb. white chocolate, cut in small pieces
3 eggs
1 t. vanilla extract
3/4 c. light corn syrup
1/4 c. butter, melted
1/2 c. Brazil nuts, chopped
1/2 c. cashews, chopped

Preheat the oven to 280°F. Grease a 10-inch springform pan. Sprinkle the graham cracker crumbs into the pan Move the pan side to side to spread the crumbs around the bottom and sides of the pan. Discard any excess crumbs.

In a double boiler, over medium heat, melt the white chocolate, stirring often. Do not heat longer than necessary. Set aside. In a medium mixing bowl, combine the eggs, vanilla and the corn syrup. Beat together thoroughly. Add the melted chocolate, butter, Brazil nuts and the cashews to the egg mixture. Mix well.

Pour the batter into the prepared pan. Bake for 1 hour 15 minutes, until the torte is golden brown and the sides begin to pull away from the pan. Remove the pan from the oven and cool for 1½ hours, then remove the sides from the pan. Serve the torte warm or chilled. Serves 16.

Enticing Maple-Glazed Biscotti

Biscotti:
2 c. all-purpose flour
1 t. baking powder
1/4 t. salt
1/4 c. butter, softened
1/2 c. sugar
1/2 c. brown sugar, firmly packed
2 eggs
1 t. maple extract
3/4 c. pecans, finely chopped

Glaze:
1 c. powdered sugar
1 T. butter, softened
1/2 t. maple flavoring
4 to 5 t. milk

Preheat the oven to 350°F. In a small bowl, stir together the flour, baking powder and the salt. Set aside.

In a large mixing bowl, combine the butter, sugar and the brown sugar on medium speed until well mixed. Add eggs, one at a time, beating after each addition. Add the maple extract and mix until smooth. Stir in the pecans. Gently stir in the flour mixture just until the dough is blended.

Divide the dough in half. On a lightly floured board roll and stretch each portion into a 12" x 1½" log. Place each log on a lightly greased cookie sheet. Bake for 25 to 30 minutes until the logs begin to crack. Remove the logs from the heat and cool for 15 to 20 minutes. Reduce the oven to 300°F. Place the cooled logs on a cutting board. Using a serrated knife, cut each log diagonally into ½-inch slices. Lay the slices, cut side down, on the cookie sheet and bake for 10 to 15 minutes. Turn the biscotti over once, during this cooking time. Cool the biscotti on wire racks.

In a small bowl, combine the powdered sugar, butter and the maple flavoring until smooth. Continue beating on low speed and add enough milk to create the glaze consistency. Dip the top edge of each cooled biscotti into the glaze. Place the glazed biscotti on waxed paper lined cookie sheets and chill until the glaze has hardened, about 1 hour. Store the biscotti in an airtight container. Makes 3 dozen biscotti.

Decadent Flourless Chocolate Cake

- 12 oz. semi-sweet or bittersweet chocolate, coarsely chopped
- 1/4 c. brewed espresso
- 4 large eggs, at room temperature
- 2 large egg yolks, at room temperature
- 1/3 c. sugar
- Pinch of salt
- 3/4 c. heavy cream
- Powdered sugar for dusting

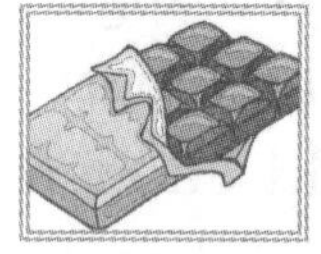

Preheat the oven to 350°F. Set the oven rack in the lower third of the oven. Line a 9-inch round cake pan with waxed paper. In a large heatproof bowl placed in hot water, melt the chocolate with the coffee, stirring until smooth. Remove from the heat and keep the mixture warm.

In a large mixing bowl, whisk the eggs, yolks and the sugar until combined. Place this in a warm bowl or skillet of hot water and whisk constantly until the eggs are very warm to the touch and the sugar is dissolved, about 2 minutes. Remove from the water and beat the egg mixture on high speed until it is cool and light and fluffy, about 3 minutes.

In a medium bowl whip the cream until it forms soft peaks. Add one-third of the egg mixture to the warm chocolate mixture and fold in until almost blended. Fold in the remaining egg mixture in two more additions. Now fold in half of the whipped cream until almost blended, and then fold in the remaining whipped cream until the mixture is evenly colored. Spread the batter into the cake pan. Place the cake pan in a large roasting pan.

Place the roasting pan into the oven and then pour water into the roasting pan until the water is half-way up the sides of the cake pan. Bake for 1½ hours until the top is firm to the touch. Transfer the pan to a wire rack and cool for 20 to 30 minutes. Invert the cake onto a serving platter and peel off the waxed paper. Cool completely. Cover with plastic wrap and chill for at least 2 hours.

To serve, let the cake stand at room temperature for 1 hour, dust the top with powdered sugar and slice into small wedges. Serves 12.

Mexican Wedding Cookies

1 c. unsalted butter, softened
1 c. powdered sugar
2 t. vanilla extract
2 c. all-purpose flour
1 c. chopped walnuts or pecans
Powdered sugar for coating the cookies

Preheat the oven to 350°F. In a large mixing bowl with an electric mixer, beat the butter until it is light and fluffy. Add the powdered sugar in increments and then add the vanilla. Beat until this mixture is light and fluffy. Add the flour, beating until well-blended. Stir in the chopped nuts.

Form the dough into 1-inch balls and place these on ungreased cookie sheets. Bake for 12 to 15 minutes until the cookies are a pale golden. Remove the cookies from the oven and let them cool on the baking sheets for 5 minutes. Transfer the cookies to wire racks to finish cooling.

Roll each cookie in the powdered sugar to coat. Store in an airtight container. Makes 40 cookies.